Rock Star?

How to Create Music, Get Gigs, and Maybe Even Make it BIG!

Written by **Stephen Anderson**
Designed and illustrated by **Zachary Snyder**
Introduction by **Eric Stefani**

BEY
WOR
Publishing

Published by
Beyond Words Publishing, Inc.
20827 NW Cornell Road
Hillsboro, Oregon 97124
503-531-8700
www.beyondword.com

This book is dedicated to all the family and friends who helped make dreams come true.
—Stephen

The information contained in this book is intended to be educational and not for diagnosis, prescription, or treatment of mental and/or physical health disorders, whatsoever. This information should not replace competent medical and/or psychological care. The authors and publisher are in no way liable for any use or misuse of the information.

ISBN: 1-885223-99-4

Editors: Marianne Monson-Burton and Michelle Roehm
Design and illustration: Zachary Snyder
Proofreader: Joseph Siegel

Printed in the United States of America
Distributed to the book trade by Publishers Group West

Library of Congress Cataloging-in-Publication Data
Anderson, Stephen.
        So, you wanna be a rock star? : how to create music, get gigs, and
    maybe even make it big / written by Stephen Anderson ; illustrated
    by Zachary Snyder.
            p.   cm.
        Summary: A guide for breaking into the music industry, discussing
    how to select an instrument, plan a budget, put together a band,
    rehearse your music, get performing gigs, and get discovered.
    Profiles kid bands who have actually performed.
        ISBN 1-885223-99-4 (paper)
        1. Rock music—Vocational guidance—Juvenile literature.
    [1. Rock music—Vocational guidance. 2. Musicians. 3. Vocational
    guidance.] I. Snyder, Zachary, ill. II. Title.
    ML3795.A828 1999
    781.66'023'73—dc21   98-52673
                                                                     CIP
                                                                  MN AC

The corporate mission of Beyond Words Publishing, Inc: *Inspire to Integrity*

A Thank You from the Editor

This book is the result of many people's dreams. When we received Stephen's idea for a book that would teach kids about the music business, we wanted it to encourage kids' dreams and give them the information they needed to make those dreams come true. But we also knew the book would never work if readers didn't believe that it could really happen to *them*. That is why we decided to get help from real-life kid bands.

We held a *So, You Wanna Be A Rockstar* contest, which was publicized everywhere. We couldn't believe the response! Entries from bands of every kind poured in. We had so much fun reading about the bands and listening to their demo tapes. It was very hard to choose the winners, but the results are the kid bands you will find profiled throughout the book. As you read about the bands, remember that they are ordinary kids just like *you*! They love creating great music by themselves and with their friends.

A huge thank you goes to all the kids who entered our contest. Thank you for taking the risk to send your songs to us. If you didn't win, don't give up. Let this book give you ideas and let the kids in the book inspire you to keep trying until you get your break. Thanks go to all the people who made this book happen, including Michelle Roehm, Amanda Hornby, Erin Doty, Meegan Thompson, and Abby Monson. A big thank you to Eric Stefani for being willing to share his incredible experience with the world.

To all the future rock stars, we wish you all the best with your music experience. Believe in yourself, trust in your musical dreams, and *anything* can happen!

—Marianne Monson-Burton

Table of Contents

Real Kid Rock Stars

Introduction

Eric Stefani of No Doubt

GWEN STEFANI   **ERIC STEFANI**

Name: Eric Stefani—I started the band No Doubt with my sister, Gwen Stefani. I was the songwriter and keyboard player in the band.

Hobbies: Playing music, animating, reading, and writing.

Pet peeve: A drummer who plays too loud!

Dream: To write great songs you want to hear over and over again.

Early Beginnings: Growing up, Gwen and I always loved music. Our parents both played instruments and they really encouraged us. I remember sitting around the piano when she was 15 and I was 17. I wrote songs and then I would ask her to come and sing them. She had a great voice and I always loved to hear my labored-over melodies sung so smoothly. She brought so much personality and life to the songs I wrote.

In high school we got together with another brother and sister team who played the drums and the bass. Together we performed in the school talent show. That was the first public performance for Gwen and me, and we loved being on the stage.

Forming the band: Later we met up with the other musicians that helped define No Doubt. Tony Kanal played bass and started getting us shows locally. Tom Dumont came in and was the best guitar player we had ever heard! Adrian Young joined when our drummer quit.

Discovered!: Not in my wildest dreams did I ever think No Doubt would reach the success that it has today. The band went through many changes to reach the point it is at now.

We played together for years before we finally got the interest of a record company. We made an album from our best songs and they put it out! It was a dream come true! We even got to make a video which was played on our local cable TV and we went on tour to support the record. We sold T-shirts at our shows and began to get a following of kids from up and down California.

Tough times: Then we hit some problems, though. The record company told us that we didn't have any songs they could play on the radio. Even though we felt like our songs were great, we were still willing to improve. So we worked really hard. We met with different producers and learned how to structure songs, edit, and record properly. By the time we had been with the record company for three years I had to go back to my old job, but Gwen didn't give up. She decided to release the CD herself. She took the songs that we had recorded as demos in our garage and mixed them. Then she made a picture collage of us for the artwork.

Sweet success: I will never forget the day I was driving home from work and I heard our song, "Just a Girl," on the radio. I couldn't believe it! I was so overwhelmed that I had to pull over and just listen. It took No Doubt ten years before we made it to the radio, but it finally came together with lots of hard work and persistence. Our individual belief in ourselves, in one another, and in the band itself really made it all happen. It was a team effort—a network of people who loved and believed in what they were doing.

My advice to young musicians today: Never lose sight of your dreams or your love for the music. Get ahold of recording equipment as soon as you can. We sold demos and T-shirts at our shows in order to buy better equipment. Listening to your recordings will inspire you to keep improving and working hard. There will be discouraging times, but never give up. I remember recording "Don't Speak." We had to rewrite the verse many times over the course of three years—very frustrating! But it paid off when that song was one of the most-played songs of 1997! The creative process can be very tedious, but your hours will pay off if you keep focused and work hard. It all comes down to believing in yourself and not giving up!

CHAPTER ONE

What's It Like to Be a Rock Star?

A Night You'll Never Forget

A hush comes over the noisy crowd as the stage lights go down. They know it's almost time for your band to play. You and your best friends are backstage waiting for the roadies to signal that everything is ready, then you head across the darkened stage with only the glow of the chrome on the drum kit lighting your way. You pick up your electric guitar and switch your amp off standby. Your heart is pounding with excitement. Somebody way in the back of the crowd shouts your band's name, and soon the whole crowd is rowdy, chanting for you to start.

The drummer hits her sticks together four times and you launch into your first—and still favorite—hit song.

The bright lights make it hard to see the crowd, but you can tell they're on their feet, loving your music. You smile at your drummer in spite of your best efforts to stay cool. This is just too much fun! The whole band is grinning, as you realize this is your dream come true. You made it!

Two hours and two encores later, you sign autographs for your eager fans until your manager signals it's time to board your tour bus. He has good news: your music video made it into the top ten today! You can't wait to get to the hotel to watch yourselves on TV.

You don't wonder how you made your dream come true. You haven't forgotten all the hard work, the people who helped you, the years of school, and the countless hours of practice. But your dream was worth the price. You and your friends will never forget this amazing night. . . .

You are a rock star!

JUSTIN   HANNAH   NICK

justincase

Our Grand Prize Winning Band!

Band Members: This awesome alternative rock and pop band is made up of three dedicated siblings! The band includes songwriter **Justin Tosco** (age 15) on guitar and vocals, brother **Nick** (age 13) on drums and percussion, and sister **Hannah** (age 12) on bass guitar and keyboard.

The Band: This is one musical family. The band's managers are their parents, who are music teachers and songwriters themselves. The kids have pretty much been a band since birth, but they have been performing professionally for the last two years in and around Charlotte, North Carolina.

This talented group got their start when Justin began learning the guitar at age 6. Then Hannah started the piano around the same age. Nick didn't want to be left out, so he started banging on pots and pans until he received his first drum set at the age of 8. The band has been jamming together ever since and they practice daily in the family garage. Justin is also a talented writer, but he wasn't interested in writing until he realized that he could apply it to their music.

This family band has had great success playing many local gigs. They have also had great experiences at large festivals such as Springfest, Festival in the Park, and Rayfest, where they played for 500 people for two hours! The Matthews Alive Festival was one of their favorite gigs. The stage was perfect, the equipment incredible, and they played for two hours in front of 700 people. They were also invited back the next year.

One of their greatest moments was winning first

place in the Honey Nut Cheerios' Battle of the Bands; they were awarded a $1,000 scholarship to the Community School of the Arts. Part of the award also included free tickets to the Sweet Sounds of Soul tour, where they were backstage guests. They got to talk to the guitar techs and road crew, go on the tour bus, and meet the Isley Brothers and Earth, Wind, and Fire!

Our Greatest Experience: Recording our music in a professional recording studio. We have just released our first CD, *Viewpoint*, which includes all original material. Justincase has now written over 30 original songs! We are grateful to our parents for support and inspiration.

Our Worst Experience: One formal gig where the audience was all over age 50 and they seemed to prefer beach music over rock music.

JUSTINCASE

Band's Dream: To sign a record contract and go on a major tour.

Congratulations, justincase! You're on your way!

Advice to Others: You have to have a love for the music. Let the music come from you and be true to yourself. Attend all the concerts you can and always learn from others.

JUSTINCASE

CHAPTER TWO

All You Have to
Do Is Dream

Do you really wanna be a rock star? Well, you can make your dream a reality. It doesn't matter where you live, what you look like, or what other people think of you. You can make your music dream come true! But it won't always be easy. Anything this great is full of hard work and sacrifices . . . but it is also a lot of fun. Have you got what it takes to make it? Take our quiz and find out.

SO, YOU WANNA BE A ROCK STAR? QUIZ

Circle the answers that best describe you:

1. One of my favorite things to do is . . .

a) listen to music. I love singing all the words, dancing around my bedroom, and air-guitaring like a fool.

b) collect stamps. I get especially excited about stamps with the U.S. presidents on them. President Harding is my favorite. He rocks!

c) help out at the local bingo night. It's so much fun!

2. I'm looking for a career that lets me have . . .

a) my very own pocket protector to hold my ruler, calculator, and pencils.

b) adventure, fun with my friends, creativity, fame, and the adoration of just about everyone I know.

c) monkeys, monkeys, monkeys. All I want is a job with monkeys.

3. Here's what I'm willing to do to make my dream come true:

a) I'll just keep lip-synching in front of my mirror and trying on lots of cool outfits until I'm ready for my big break.

b) I'll get an electric guitar and jam until everyone knows how great I am and a record company sends me a million dollars to make a CD.

c) I'll take music lessons so I can learn how to really play an instrument, I'll sacrifice time with my friends so I can practice and rehearse with my band, and I'll do well in school so my parents will support my dream and won't kill me.

If you really want to be a rock star, the correct answers are: 1, a; 2, b; 3, c. If you got all these right, you are on your way! In the coming pages, you'll find practically all the information you'll need for your future in music, whether you want a career or just some great experiences. You'll also meet some inspiring teen bands who are already performing for crowds. If you circled any of the wrong answers, you're a very unusual person. But that's okay, there's hope even for you—the world of rock music is full of weird people. In fact, most rock stars are a bit strange, aren't they?

One of the best things about music is that there's room for everybody. You can start anywhere and along the way you can develop the skills and talents that you need to succeed. There are many kinds of music out there, so you have lots of options to choose from. You may love country, hip-hop, swing, jazz, R&B, alternative, ska, rap, or bluegrass. Maybe you will even invent your own kind of music! Whatever you love, you can make it big—and you can have a great time doing it!

Another great thing about choosing a career in music is that you have lots of time. Just look at the Rolling Stones . . . they're *really old* and they still play to fans all over the world! They've been together for almost 40 years. As a musician today, you have opportunities that bands in the past never had. When the Rolling Stones started their band, personal computers weren't invented yet, and nobody had even *dreamed* of the Internet! You have access to all the information you need for making the right decisions along the way. You just need to know where to find it.

Now, let's talk about *you*! One of your favorite subjects, right? Here's another reason you are uniquely suited to music—you are unique! There has never been anyone exactly like you, so you are the only one who can write a song about *your* view of the world. You'll even meet other teens like you who are writing and recording their own songs *right now*. But first you need to build a foundation for your career.

When you want to build a house, you start with the foundation. Without a foundation your home wouldn't last very long. Your music also needs a strong foundation, if you really want to be a rock star. For some stars, their foundation starts with their family. *What if my home life is lousy?* you may ask. *Does that mean I can't do it?* No, that just means you may have to work harder at building a foundation by yourself. But don't worry, you're not alone. Lots of rock stars make it on their own. And it could be worse. You could have been born in Payson, Utah!

Now, there's nothing wrong with Payson, Utah—really. It's just a long way from the music meccas of Los Angeles and New York. What are your chances of becoming a rock star in Payson, Utah? *Then* imagine that your parents move you even further away from fame . . . to Alaska! You grow up in the Alaskan wilderness—no electricity, no indoor plumbing, no TV! On top of this, your parents get divorced and you're really poor. What a life! Sound like a good foundation for a music career? Well, that's how Jewel grew up. In her late teens she moved to San Diego . . . but she was so broke she had to live in her VW van while she played in coffeehouses. At age twenty-three her first record went platinum—a rock star's dream come true!

How about Elvis Presley—the *King* of Rock 'n' Roll? Elvis was born in a one-room shack in rural Mississippi, and during his early childhood his father was in prison. Young Elvis was so shy that by the time he recorded his first record the only audience he had performed in front of was his bedroom mirror!

John Rzeznik, the lead singer of the Goo Goo Dolls, was born into a poor Polish immigrant family. Both his parents died when he was 15 years old, so his four older sisters raised him and encouraged his musical passion. He was in several different punk bands until they were discovered while playing in a small local club. Look at them now!

Then there's Jakob Dylan of the Wallflowers. Instead of relying on the name of Bob Dylan, his father, to boost his career, he didn't tell anybody who he was! He toured anonymously with his band for seven years, playing in any dive that would take them, perfecting their songs until their music was ready for the big time. Jakob *truly* made it on his own.

And what about you? Do you come from humble beginnings? Do you have a shaky foundation for a music career? Is your family poor? Do you live in the middle of nowhere? Are you the only person in your town who likes music? Adversity might make your dream more difficult to achieve, but whatever challenges you face, you can do it. Hard work, dedication, and believing in your dream will take you *anywhere* you want to go.

When you get the blues, feel down, and are ready to quit your dream, think about the Goo Goo Dolls, Jewel, Elvis, and all the famous rock stars who had their own struggles on their way to the top. If they can do it, so can you!

ANTHONY   ROSEZETTA   DARIUS

The DRU Band

First Place Winner

Band Members: The DRU band (Darius and Rosezetta Upshaw band) started performing in 1995 and features three of the hottest young jazz/blues musicians on the scene today. The band includes **Darius Upshaw** (age 14) on guitar (he also plays bass, sax, piano, and drums), his

sister **Rosezetta** (age 12) on electric bass (she also plays stand-up bass, guitar, and clarinet), and their friend **Anthony Duarte** (age 13) on drums. In addition to being one of the best drummers in the San Francisco area, Anthony also plays conga and percussion.

The Band: The DRU Band has had many great experiences and honors. B.B. King once told Darius, "One day, you'll be the best guitar player around." Rosezetta attends the Young Musicians Program for the gifted at UC Berkeley! And Anthony has been featured in several drum magazines as one of the top young drummers in the Bay Area. Together this rockin' group has been performing about 80 shows a year since 1995. They have played at the California State Fair (where they took third place), local jazz clubs, the California Blues Festival (in front of 2,000 people!), the Shoreline Jazz Festival, the Monterey Blues Festival, and the San Francisco Jazz Festival.

The DRU Band has also played at prestigious hotels such as the Ritz Carlton and the Fairmont. One time when they were playing at the California Blues Festival, a representative from the Blues and R&B Foundation came onto the stage and presented The DRU Band with a trophy for "keeping the blues alive." They were also recently presented with the San Francisco Bay Area Entertainer's Top Star Award for the Most Promising Young Artists.

Our Greatest Experience: When we played at two San Francisco Giants games. Afterwards we were invited to watch the game from the team's luxury suite!

A Crazy Experience: According to Rosezetta: Just before our turn to play at the Monterey Blues Festival, a bee stung my arm! It hurt a lot, and when it was our turn to go on I was still mad, but I decided not to let a bee ruin my performance. So on my Brick House solo, I got loose! When I got off the stage, the crowd went wild—they loved it! Later when we were walking back to the car, I saw the bee lying on the ground. I was about to stomp on it, but my dad said, "Save that bee—we should sting you before every performance!"

Band's Dream: To have a long and successful career in the music business.

Advice to Others: Work hard and learn everything that you can, but most of all have fun and enjoy what you are doing. Support the other kids who are in bands locally. If you work together you will all get a lot further!

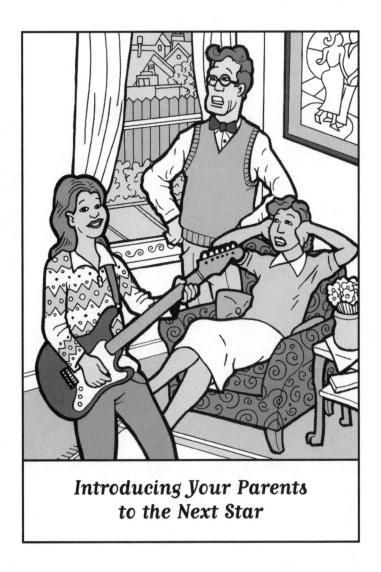

CHAPTER THREE

Introducing Your Parents to the Next Star

So, you've decided you *do* want to be a rock star. Or at least you want to give it a shot and have a great time playing music with your friends. Before you can do much else, you have to get your parents on board. Your life will be much easier if you can get them on your side in making your dream come true. Just busting out with, "Mom, Dad, guess what? I want to be a rock star! Isn't that great?" probably won't work.

Convincing them that you want to play an instrument may be easy, or it may be hard. Imagine the look on their faces if you told them you actually *want* to take piano lessons. They'd probably be thrilled, thinking, *Hey, maybe she'll be a famous classical pianist someday!* Now imagine telling them you want to be a drummer. Do you see them screaming, *"Save us! Save us!"* while running from the house?

Here are some tips for getting your parents to see the light. But first, think of what might be worrying them:

• You won't keep up in school, you'll drop out of all after-school activities, and you'll fail all your classes.

• You're going to be up all night making a horrible racket.

• You're going to get into drugs and alcohol and ruin your life.

• You'll never clean your room again.

• You'll get involved with really weird people.

• You'll become famous and forget all about them.

Just kidding. But it probably wouldn't hurt to tell them all about the big house you'll buy them when you're rich and famous, and the hit songs you'll write about what supportive parents they have been.

So, that's what they're thinking. All you can do is promise not to fulfill their worst nightmares, and then keep your promises. Your best weapon is to discipline yourself. For example, instead of waiting to be told that your room needs to be cleaned, do it ahead of time. Hey, try being extra helpful around the house every once in a while. This probably sounds like bad news for you, but at least put in 100 percent in the beginning, when your parents are most likely to say "Forget it!" You can go back to a normal pace after they've gotten used to your being in a band. Who knows? Maybe they'll become your biggest fans!

Another great way to show your parents that you're mature enough to join a band is to write and sign a contract. In the contract, promise to keep up on your schoolwork and other activities. Promise to continue doing your chores on time and to hold practices and rehearsals at a decent hour. Promise to stay away from drugs and alcohol. Agree on consequences that will happen if you don't keep your promises (but that won't happen, right?), and you might even be able to sneak in some rewards for keeping your end of the bargain. Give your parents a reason to believe in you. You may be amazed at how they respond to the "new you."

The Miraculous Mozart Effect

As a last ditch option, try this one on your parents. Have you ever heard of the Mozart Effect? It's one of the best reasons for learning music. Research has shown that if you study music, you will do better in school and even get smarter!

It turns out that any complex music, even rock music, causes the brain to react in a positive way and increases your "higher brain function." Try that phrase out on your parents if they're not excited about your rock star aspirations. And if they see you doing better in school and think it may be the Mozart Effect in action, *of course* they'll be more willing to support your music dreams. Who doesn't want their kid to have "higher brain function"?

Jeff Simo

Second Place Winner

About Jeff: Jeff Simo is only 13 years old, but he has already had more musical experience than many musicians twice his age! He has played the guitar for nine years (over 640 guitar lessons!) and he also plays the piano. He loves Rock 'n' Roll, Blues, Rockabilly, Soul, Country, and Pop music.

History: Jeff is an incredibly musical guy! He started the guitar in kindergarten and was performing publicly by the age of 7. This guitar virtuoso got his start playing as a well-respected Elvis impersonator and credits Elvis's strong personality for his love of entertaining. By the age of 9 he was performing regularly at Harrah's Casino and Chicago White Sox Comisky Park. Another honor came in his being chosen to play lead guitar in 22 sold-out performances of the musical *Grease*. However, his largest performance so far was in front of 3,000 people at the Civic Center Plaza in Phoenix! The media has paid lots of attention to Jeff, and he has been featured by WGN television, the Chicago Tribune, FOX news, CBS television, and the Arizona Tribune—to name only a few.

Jeff is now considered to be a college-level guitar player and he studies with a tutor from Arizona State University. One night he attended a jam night of The Blues Sevilles and was given a chance to perform. He did such a great job on lead guitar that they offered him a weekly slot. Recently, Jeff has decided to take his music in a new direction by starting a band. He has begun working with a bass player and a drummer. Their group will be known as the Millennium Man Band.

JEFF SIMO

My Greatest Experience: The 1994 Elvis Fantasy Fest in Indiana, where I performed for Elvis's right-hand man, Joe Esposito. Joe gave my show rave reviews and we still keep in touch.

My Worst Experience: One performance at the school talent show where a plug went faulty and my electric guitar amp went out. I was embarrassed but I knew that the show must go on! I picked up my acoustic guitar and finished the song.

Dream: To bring the past 50 years of music into the next 50 years and the new millennium with my original songs.

Advice to Others: You've always got to strive for excellence and never believe that you are doing the best you can do. Practice every free moment and explore different avenues of music.

JEFF SIMO

CHAPTER FOUR

Finding Your Instrument

Rock music is a unique American art form with humble beginnings. It began way back in the '40s and '50s, when teenagers didn't have any music of their own. Parents pretty much decided what was on the radio—big band music or Frank Sinatra. You can imagine the torture. When rock 'n' roll did sneak onto the radio, many parents forbade their kids from listening to this "devil music." But the power of rock was too strong.

In 1955 rock 'n' roll finally invaded the radio waves with Bill Haley and his Comets' hit, "Rock Around the Clock." The other founders of rock 'n' roll—Elvis Presley, Chuck Berry, and Little Richard—soon followed. Finally there was music for teens. It wasn't long before these same guys and girls got ahold of their own guitars, drums, pianos, and just about anything they could make music with . . . and the rest is rock history.

Since that time music has become very diverse and now there are many different kinds of music that you can play. Do you want to add your own chapter to the history of music? Then you'd better start learning an instrument! Just about any instrument can be played in rock music—saxophone, flute, trombone, trumpet, violin, cello, vibes, accordion, harmonica, spoons. The list goes on and on. John Lennon of the Beatles even played the harpsichord in one of their songs!

But what should you learn to play *first*? Have you seen any bands led by flute players lately? I didn't think so. The more instruments you can play, the more valuable you will be to your band, but the four instruments called the **Quartet**—the piano, guitar, bass guitar, and drums—are the basic instruments you need for any type of band. You'll be in good shape if you learn one of these to begin with.

Should I Play the Piano?

Why would anyone want to take piano lessons? You might think that the piano is something your parents make you do . . .

something for old people . . . definitely not something for a future rock star. Right? Wrong!

Here are some cool secrets about the piano that you might not know:

• It's a lot easier to find a band that needs a piano player. Guitar players are a dime a dozen, since there are about 15 million guitar players in the U.S. And they're all looking for a band to play in. That's a lot of competition for guitar players.

• Do you want to learn to sing? The acoustic piano is the easiest instrument to use when you're learning to sing.

• The best reason for choosing the piano as your instrument is that it's the easiest for learning to read and write music. And reading and writing music is crucial if you want to be a songwriter. On piano, musical notes and the relationships between them are easy to see, while on guitar they're much more difficult to figure out. Most guitar players never learn to read music. Almost *all* piano players do.

ROCK STAR SECRET #1:

Piano lessons are one of the best shortcuts ever
for learning to play and write rock music!

What Kind of Piano Should I Learn to Play?

Notice I'm using the word "piano," not "keyboard." Although most rock bands today have electronic keyboards instead of pianos, I recommend you learn the old-fashioned, no-plug-in kind first. There are a million sounds and rhythms built into an electronic keyboard and it's almost impossible not to mess around with it all day. Instead of learning to play and read music, you'll probably just fool around. Your parents and band-mates won't be impressed and it'll take you that much longer to become a rock star.

Also, since most electric pianos have shorter keyboards than acoustic pianos, the keys don't have the proper action you need to learn to play. If you learn the fundamentals on a real piano with a teacher, then when you buy an electric keyboard you'll be ready to use it. There's going to be plenty of time for you to play with cool keyboard sounds *after* you master the basics.

Should I Play the Guitar?

When you think of a rock band, the guitar is probably the first thing you notice. It's usually the loudest and hardest to ignore. When adults want a band to "stop all the noise," they usually mean the guitar player! The world has been crazy about guitars for years—*hundreds* of years, in fact. Guitars have been around even longer than pianos.

Are you ready for some great guitar news? In all those hundreds of years, there has never been a better time to learn the guitar. Never. Guitars are more affordable now than ever before. To buy a good guitar you don't need to work for years—a summer may be enough. Plus, there are tons of guitar styles, colors, and shapes to fit everyone, in almost any price range. There are also great books and videos that will help you learn practically any style of guitar playing you can imagine. And high quality guitar teachers can be found, no matter where you live.

How Do I Choose a Guitar?

Here's some sound advice for choosing the best guitar. Pick a guitar that's easy for you to play and sounds good—so you will love playing it. This is really important, because when you're starting out, your fingers will hurt a lot, but the love of music will carry you through.

Speaking of help, it's great to get advice from an expert. He or she can show you which guitars are easy to play. That person can be the owner of your local music store or a friend who's played the guitar for a while. Don't be afraid to ask for help. You want to spend your money on the best guitar for you!

You can buy a guitar from a catalog or off the Internet, but I recommend going to a music store because:

• No matter how wonderful they look in the slick magazine pictures, you need to actually play a guitar to know if it fits you.

• If something goes wrong with your guitar, a music store can help you fix it and maybe even give you a loaner until yours is repaired.

• As your playing gets better and you are ready for a challenge, you'll want to upgrade your guitar. A music store can give you a trade-in to help you afford the next step. One store owner we talked to remembers a customer who upgraded to a better guitar six times in one year! That guy practiced hours and hours every day. Now that's dedication!

Electric or Acoustic?

When you're just beginning, the best choice of guitar is the one that's easiest to play and one that you can afford. An acoustic guitar is the best choice when you are starting out because:

• You can take an acoustic guitar with you anywhere, since you don't have to plug it into an amplifier. When you're learning to play, you *should* take your guitar everywhere so you can practice and get used to playing in front of people. Your fingers need to be broken in every day.

- Acoustic guitars are better for songwriting. Just ask Bob Dylan, Jewel, or Tom Petty. They all use acoustic guitars for songwriting, even though they also own the best electric guitars!

- Do you want to learn to sing? The acoustic guitar is the second best instrument to use when learning to sing (after the piano).

- If you learn on an acoustic guitar, you will then be able to play any electric guitar. You'll be glad you learned acoustic first.

If you *do* have your heart set on an electric guitar, consider a compromise. There are now many acoustic/electric guitars. They sound fine with or without an amp. It's not as good as starting out on a regular acoustic guitar, but it's better than beginning with only an electric guitar.

New or Used?

The brand of guitar is not very important when you're starting out. Buy the best quality you can afford, so when you want to trade it in for a better guitar, your investment will pay off. But it makes the most sense to buy a used guitar first. Why? Two reasons:

- You may decide the guitar isn't for you because at the start your fingers get really sore. Some people decide the guitar is more difficult than it looks and try something else.

- Since so many people quit, there are *thousands* of affordable, used guitars to choose from. It's easy to find one that's perfect for you.

Right- or Left-Handed?

Whether you are right-handed or left-handed, learn to play the guitar with your right hand strumming. This is very important because it's much easier to learn the chord forms when the left hand does the fingering. If you learn right-handed strumming, you will be able to play 99% of the guitars you encounter at jam sessions, music stores, etc. You will also be able to play the fingering for all the other stringed instruments such as the violin, cello, and double bass.

Should I Play the Bass?

The heart of music is the "rhythm section"—the bass guitar and the drums. These days most bands use an electric bass, but in the early years most players used the double bass (also called a stand-up bass). The double bass is still used in orchestras, blues bands, and even in some rock and swing bands like the Brian Stetzer Orchestra, the Cherry Poppin' Daddies, and the Mighty Mighty Bosstones.

Should you learn to play bass? There are lots of good reasons to give this instrument a try:

• The best thing is that you will *always* be able to find someone to play with. Good bass players are always in demand. When you play the bass well, you can work in any style of music, just about any night, in any city.

• Bass players are often the most creative musicians in a band and usually have the most steady, reliable personalities.

• If you're going to be a songwriter, you need a working knowledge of the bass. Often a good bass rhythm will give you a good song idea.

• The bass player and drummer are the key to a great band. They keep the beat steady and create a lot of a band's sound. When the rhythm section drives a band, fans truly *feel* the music.

Electric or Double Bass?

Double basses are *really* expensive, so buying one just to see if you like playing bass is not practical. Non-electric basses have a unique sound and are worth learning for the experience. If you're interested, try one out at your school or community orchestra.

Not too long ago, an electric bass and amplifier were an expensive investment for the beginning bass player. But now there are electric basses available for just about every budget. The electric bass guitar and amp are also much easier to pack around than the double bass, which requires a small van or station wagon. The case for a double bass is big enough to sleep in!

Should I Play the Drums?

Compared to the piano and guitar, drums are ancient. Actually they've been used for music and communication as long as humans have been around. But are they for you? The three reasons most people decide not to play drums are:
- They're the most expensive instrument in a band.
- They're heavy and difficult to pack around.
- They're big and noisy—difficult to practice in a house.

But, there are some great reasons why drums might be the perfect instrument for you:
- Are you a born leader? The drummer is in ultimate control of the band—they're in the driver's seat! In fact, the drum seat is often called the "throne." The drummer starts the song so that everyone can feel the tempo, holds the beat steady through the entire number, and then finishes the song with a bang that everyone will remember. *Very* cool.
- Good drummers are always in demand, since they're pretty rare. Most kids try shortcuts to learning the drums, instead of mastering the basics first. A drummer who can keep a steady beat, no matter what style of music, and can play quiet or loud without losing the

rhythm will always have a band to play in.

• Playing the drums is very *physical*. It's a great way to vent bad feelings, while expressing yourself in a creative, positive way!

What Kind of Drum Set Do I Want?

Are you strong? Drummers have the heaviest gear to pack around—all the hardware and stands will give you muscles fast! So, keep your drum kit simple. Four-piece sets are very cool. A snare drum, small tom, floor tom, and bass drum are all you really need. You'll want cymbals eventually, but you don't need them when you're first learning to play.

Should I Buy a Drum Set?

The drum set is the most expensive instrument in a rock band. It's hard to find a good set of drums for under $1,000, new *or* used. You need some expert advice when you're ready to buy your first set (see next chapter).

One place you can get free experience on a full set is in your school band program. If you're serious about playing drums, ask your school music teacher if you can join the drum section. That way you can learn to read music, keep a rhythm, get familiar with the drum hardware, and decide how much you like drumming, before you spend a lot of money.

Another good thing to do before spending a lot of money on a drum set is to take some lessons. When you're ready to start your lessons, buy a tunable practice pad (about $25) and a decent pair of drumsticks (about $10). Even if you're left-handed, learn right-handed to start because nine out of ten drumsets will be set up right-handed. If you decide you love drumming, buy an electronic metronome with an earphone—this will help you learn to keep perfect time. When you want more sounds, set up cardboard boxes and plastic buckets of different sizes and shapes to practice on. Even before you invest in a set of drums, you can have a blast practicing. *And* your parents will see that you're serious about it.

What About Music Lessons?

Be sure to save some of your hard-earned money for music lessons. If you want to be a real rock star, you will definitely need them. But, how can you recognize a good teacher? Ask them some questions:

- Will you teach me different styles?
- Can I record our lessons?
- Will you teach me a mix of reading music and playing by ear?
- Did you go to school?
- How long have you been playing?
- How long have you been teaching?

Make sure you find someone who can teach you good fundamentals. It's not so important that they play the exact style of music you love. It's more important to find someone who can play lots of styles. If you're going to be a songwriter, you'll want to know as many musical styles as possible. Supplement your lessons with videos and books. Music stores rent them out and your library should have a good selection of "how-to" instrument videos. Learn as many styles and techniques as you can handle.

Cristina Bautista

An Up-and-Coming Musician

About Cristina: Although Cristina is only 12 years old, she already has a firm foundation for her music career. This passionate young girl plays the acoustic guitar, electric guitar, piano, keyboard, tambourine, and bongos—oh, she also sings. Cristina loves to write and play pop/rock music with a bit of folk.

History: Cristina first decided that she wanted to be a musician when she started watching MTV somewhere around the age of 2! She decided to begin early and started taking piano lessons when she was 5. She started the guitar when she was 9, and has been jamming ever since. She practices for several hours every day and definitely has the passion to stick with it.

My Greatest Experience: Performing in my school's talent show. It was my first time on stage and I loved the feeling of performing.

Worst Experience: Unfortunately not too many kids my age are serious about music. This makes it very hard to keep a band together. I have started many bands, without success so far. That's OK—I'm going to keep perfecting my skills until I find the perfect band for me.

Dream: To start a successful band and give people great and enjoyable performances.

Advice to Others: Decide what is important to you and stay true to yourself always. Rock on!

MARTIN ALEX JACK

Two Kings and a Jack

Band Members: This incredible bluegrass band is made up of three dedicated members: **Alex Truax** (age 9) plays the banjo, **Martin Stevens** (age 10) plays the guitar, mandolin, and fiddle, and **Jack Truax** (age 11) plays the guitar and electric bass. Their coach, Chick Rose, often plays with them.

The Band: It all began when a neighbor moved away and left a banjo and a guitar behind. For a year the instruments sat in the basement, but then one day Alex and Jack picked them up and started messing around. A week later they asked for lessons. Through their teacher they met Martin, and now they practice together five hours a week, as well as several hours on their own each day. All this work has paid off, and they are in high demand! They have had paid gigs at coffee shops, rotary clubs, retirement homes, company picnics, private parties, and grocery stores. They also enjoy playing at many bluegrass festivals around Oregon. All three members have individually placed in state and regional competitions.

Our Greatest Experience: We had a really incredible performance in front of a rotary club. Everything was just perfect—the sound system, the excited audience, the instrumentals, and the harmonies. We love to perform at our best, and we also received several future bookings.

Worst Experience: One gig that we played at a big outdoor square in downtown Portland. The sound system was set up for a rock band, so it didn't come together at all. Then it started to rain really hard. Our audience practically ran away.

Band's Dream: To become one of the top bluegrass bands on the West Coast. We want to play in festivals all over the country and maybe even in Europe.

Advice to Others: Practice! We practice a lot, and we have a great time practicing so it doesn't feel like work. The more we practice the better we sound.

CHAPTER FIVE

A Rock Star on a Budget

Now that you know what's out there to learn, some of you might be thinking, *But how am I going to afford this? Buying instruments? Paying for lessons? I'm not Bill Gates, you know!* Good **point.** Learning to play an instrument can be expensive. But it can **also be** affordable, if you know what you're doing. If you're going to pursue your dream on a tight budget, there are two things you'll need: a network and some creativity.

Starting Your Network

The first thing you need on your road to stardom is a network. A network is the people you'll go to when you have questions or need advice—people who know about instruments, lessons, performing, the music industry, etc. Let's say you like playing the trumpet more than any of the Quartet instruments. Maybe you're not sure yet what you want to play, or you only want to sing. You need more information. You've got to start asking questions, exploring, and finding the players and teachers who can help you and encourage your dream.

ROCK STAR SECRET #2:

*Your success in the music business depends
on your ability to find and work
with the right people.*

Here are the kinds of people you'll want in your network:

• **Music store employees:** They're great for questions about instruments, lessons, and good deals.

• **Professional local musicians:** They're great for advice about your band, the music industry, and common mistakes. If you're lucky, they will also introduce you to people who can influence your career.

• **Music and band teachers:** They can help you find used or cheap instruments, teachers for lessons, and places to practice.

There are people all around you who will help you take your career to the top. All you have to do is find them, ask questions and pay attention. So don't be bashful—go out there and build your network!

1. You can meet local musicians by hanging out at cafes, county fairs, and anywhere else musicians play. After the show, go up and introduce yourself. If it is a casual setting, you may be able to jam together.

2. You can build your network while building your skill set. Check with local music stores to find out about music workshops and seminars. Many stores send out monthly newsletters, so make sure you are on their mailing lists.

3. Another great way to get to know some of the musicians in your area is to volunteer with a local sound system during the busy summer concert season. It's hard work, but you will meet lots of people and learn more about sound systems and lighting.

ROCK STAR SECRET #3:

People in the music industry will love answering
your questions. It is fun to talk
about what you love.

Warning: Some music store employees are paid a percentage of what they sell. They may try to pressure you into buying gear you don't need. If you think this is happening, tell them you just want the basics, not stuff you don't need. Remember, you don't need much to start. Keep it simple.

Also, keep in mind that there are people out there who may

try to take advantage of you. Keep your guard up. If in doubt, ask your parents' advice, especially when you're spending money!

Ten Ways to Find Cheap or Free Instruments

1. You might need to start out playing on school instruments. Who cares? If you're learning to read music and playing in a group, you are laying a solid foundation for your rock star future.

2. Visit the Goodwill, Salvation Army, and community thrift stores. Good instruments are donated all the time. Sometimes they need work, but they're cheap and your network can help you fix them up.

3. Let your family and friends know that you're serious about learning an instrument. You may be surprised at who will loan you that piano that's been collecting dust for years, or that guitar in the closet.

4. Ask your music or band teacher—they might know someone with an instrument to loan or sell.

5. Post notices on bulletin boards in music stores, coffeehouses, clubs, and anywhere else where musicians would go.

6. Check your local newspaper's classified and nickel ads.

7. Ask the people who work in your local music store.

8. If you're looking for a piano, try your church or synagogue. You could trade your labor for a chance to practice on their piano.

9. Senior centers and retirement homes usually have pianos. Maybe if you occasionally played for the people who live there, they'd let you practice on it. This can also give you experience playing in front an audience.

10. Can't afford a sound system? Offer to warm up for an established band for free in exchange for borrowing their sound system once in a while. It's another great way to get practice performing in public.

Getting Lessons Cheap or Free

• Music workshops and seminars are often reasonably priced and a great way to learn. Ask the people sponsoring the event if you could earn the price of admission by posting flyers, cleaning afterward, or moving the musicians' equipment (their least favorite job).

• Maybe a teacher has a yard that needs mowing . . . or some weekly housecleaning . . . or a pet that needs walking. Try making a trade.

• Most libraries have videos for learning different styles of music, and through interlibrary loans there are hundreds of tapes available to you.

• Check with your local community college, the park district, or YMCA. They often have great music classes at low cost.

And don't forget your birthday, Christmas, Hanukkah, Easter, even Cinquo de Mayo. Let your family know that the gifts you really want are those that will help your music dreams. There are also lots of ways to *earn* your own money for lessons and instruments. Check out the book *Better Than a Lemonade Stand: Small Business Ideas for Kids* (see Chapter 15), written by a 15-year-old. This book has tons of great money-making ideas for kids like you. Make it happen! Your dedication will reward you in the end.

Rebecca Wood

An Up-and-Coming Musician

About Rebecca: Rebecca is a 14-year-old girl from a small town in Nebraska, but she has a big dream. She wants to take her music to the top, and she has a great start. Rebecca writes and sings pop/rock music.

History: Rebecca has wanted to be a singer for as long as she can remember. She wrote her first song about her

baby-sitter when she was 6! She started getting really serious, though, a few years ago when she wrote a song called "Your Girl." When she sang it to a friend who owned a recording studio, he immediately wanted to help her. Together they recorded and mixed the song.

Rebecca wasn't content to stop there, though. She spent the summer performing her songs at talent shows throughout Nebraska. Although she was the only one who was not singing a country song, she still received a great response. Each time she performed she realized that the stage is where she wants to be. Rebecca practices several hours every day, working on voice, songwriting, or the electric guitar. She has the determination to succeed!

My Greatest Experience: The first time I recorded my original song in a recording studio. I was there with the headphones, singing harmony to my song, and then I

R E B E C C A   W O O D

listened to the playback. I kept thinking, "That's my song! I wrote that!" It was incredible.

Worst Experience: One time I was performing in a really big talent show. I was up on stage with my back to the audience waiting for the music to start. I did this dance move, spun around, and . . . stepped right on the microphone cord and broke it! It was horrible!

Dream: Right now I am an ordinary small town girl, but my dream is that someday you will come to one of my concerts or see me doing an interview on television.

Advice to Others: I never thought making it would be hard. I thought that I would go to one talent show and be discovered. But fame doesn't come easy. You have to fail many times before you succeed. Believe in yourself, follow your dreams, and don't let anyone tear you down.

R E B E C C A   W O O D

CHAPTER SIX

Starting Your Band

Band or Solo?

Guess what? You can play rock music all by yourself. Many great musicians and singers write their music by themselves and then hire everybody else to play exactly what they're told (think of

Mariah Carey, Sheryl Crow, and Ray Charles). Some solo artists even use machines for their backup bands (like Beck and White Town).

There are some benefits to going solo. You don't have to worry about arguing with your band-mates or forcing them to practice. You do everything yourself and rely only on your own abilities. Solo performers make all the decisions alone; people in a band have to lobby for the things they think are important, and they learn how to compromise.

Going solo can be a big burden, though. There's no one to lean on when the going gets tough; no one to brainstorm with and help make hard decisions. You also miss out on some of the real fun of making music! There's nothing that can replace the joy of jamming with your best friends in front of an audience that loves you! You and your band can help each other earn money and share a great adventure. When you realize your dream together, it will make your success even sweeter.

So, which suits *you* better? Only you can decide. If you decide to go solo, then become a multi-instrumentalist! Alanis Morissette plays the piano, guitar, bass, harmonica, and flute! Learn to sing, play percussion, and play either the piano or guitar so you can write your own songs. Then you can solo with authority, and when you add a band for touring, you can show them what you want them to play!

What's in a Band?

If solo's not your style, then a band it is. So, what exactly do you need to have a band? If your band is going to sound halfway decent, you need to have at least three instruments from the Quartet in your band: piano, guitar, bass, or drums. Your band must have a bass and drums, since those give your music its beat. Then, if you have only three band members, you can choose between having a lead guitar or a lead piano. If you have four band members (which is even better), you can have a guitar *and* a piano. If you want, you can have *ten* band members all playing wacky instruments—there's not really a maximum. But three instruments from the Quartet is the minimum for a band. If you don't have three people yet, don't stress. It doesn't mean that you are doomed. Build your network and you will find others eventually. In the meantime, don't give up—keep practicing!

Big Band or Small?

There are some advantages to having a small band. First of all, it's easier to make decisions and there's more money to go around when you start getting gigs. The downside is that everybody has to work harder to create a full sound. A bigger band can be more fun, plus it gives you more flexibility and creativity. But everyone has to listen carefully to the other instruments in the band or your music will sound muddy or busy.

Finding Musicians

Let's say you play the piano and you have a couple of friends who play the drums and the saxophone. You need a guitar player and a bass player. How are you going to find them? Here are some tips:

- Ask around. Your friends probably know someone who plays.
- Ask the school music teacher or your local music teacher.
- Put an ad in your school paper or the city newspaper.
- Put up flyers at music stores, coffeehouses, clubs, and other places where band-less musicians would go.

• Check with your network. Local musicians and music store employees might personally know someone looking for a band.

Finding a Lead Singer

What if your band is lacking a lead singer? While you are hanging around chorus class, remember that there are several traits you want this singer to have. First, the singer should be able to think quickly because there are always things happening that require someone to keep the crowd interested. For instance, maybe your drummer has a problem and can't play for a few minutes. You need someone who can entertain as well as sing. It's not as important that they sing perfectly, but they should have a memorable voice. Think of Bob Dylan or Lucinda Williams—their voices aren't always perfect, but they are so compelling that you remember them and enjoy their style. In a perfect world your lead singer will be great at harmonizing and will also play an instrument. Check with your school's choir teacher to find this kind of person—or maybe you are the one!

Divide the Work

Once you get a group together, it's important to decide who's going to be in charge of various band needs. Once you get to know each other better, you should decide as a group what role each member will play. For example, the player with the most outgoing personality should arrange the gigs and do most of the "front" work onstage (talk to the audience between songs, tell jokes, etc). The player who has artistic talent should design your posters. If someone's good at math, they keep track of the finances. The person with the most muscles hauls the gear onstage.

All Work and No Play . . .

Be sure to set realistic goals for your band, adjust them when you need to, and reward yourselves when you achieve them. A goal could be "We're going to rehearse ten hours a week for three months so we're ready for our performance." If you do it, treat yourselves to a pizza party. Regularly set aside time to do stuff together as a band: go camping, catch a movie, relax and have some laughs together. Remember, you're building a team that you want to last so you can make it to the top together.

Staying Friends till the End

No matter what happens with your band, you want to try to stay friends. You're going to need to communicate with each other— that means *talk.* Talk about what's going on in the band and how you're all feeling. If people just hold things in, one day someone will quit. And then what?

But band members *do* quit. People join bands for different reasons and quit for different reasons. You shouldn't expect everyone to be as dedicated as you are, so it's better to prepare for the worst. When you start your band, agree on and write down what will happen if someone leaves the band. If your band buys group equipment, keep track of what each member paid so you can refund the person who's leaving. If you're ready for changes, then they won't take you by surprise and ruin your friendships. It is important to remember that when band members leave and new people replace them, the entire band chemistry will change, so be ready to go with the flow.

What if your *worst* nightmare comes true and your whole band falls apart? It's not the end of the world. Even when your identity with a band is secure, don't forget who you are. You have your own talents, separate from the band. If the band goes bust, it's just a small glitch in your rise to stardom. You just have to start again from where you are. Don't lose sight of your dream.

Girl Rockers

Not so long ago, music was pretty much a "Boy's Club." Only a few lucky girls got in—Joni Mitchell, Janis Joplin, Bonnie Raitt, to name a few. But that's all changed now. There's a rock revolution going on. Check out the radio—women like Sarah McLachlan, Jewel, Sheryl Crow, Tori Amos, Mariah Carey, Whitney Houston, Paula Cole, Alanis Morissette, Fiona Apple, Joan Osborne, and a bunch of other great women have taken over! One of the coolest events to come out of this "girl rock" revolution is the Lilith Fair. It's one of the first and only events to give unknown new bands and singers a place to play in front of national audiences.

Thanks to these women and some other changes in the music industry, it's a whole new world for musicians now. In the past, record companies pretty much decided whose voices were heard. But with the Internet, the music business is opening up to anyone who has the talent to attract the fans. There are now Web sites that will help you sell your music directly to your fans. Rock has truly become music *of the people, by the people, and for the people.*

JULIA   *AMANDA*   *ELISE "BIZ"*

Crimson

An Up-and-Coming Band

Band Members: Some girls are obsessed with boys, others with computers, and some like shopping. But these girls are hyper-obsessed with music. Meet Crimson, a band from Colorado with musicians **Amanda Parsons** (age 13), who adores playing the drums, **Julia Hogan** (age 13) playing the guitar, and **Biz Minter** (age 13) who takes it away on bass guitar.

The Band: Although these girls have never performed in public, they had to win our contest because they have so

much love and passion for their music! And that *is* what it's all about, after all. They have been together for over a year and are addicted to their music. "I could play the drums 24/7 and never get tired of it!" Amanda yells. They play pop/rock music, but hate to be classified as a "normal" teen band, because their lyrics are much deeper. They are scheduled to perform for their school talent show coming up, which could be their big break.

Our Greatest Experience: We have written over 30 original songs, and our greatest experience was when we played the first one together. It sounded really good and we knew that we could make it!

Band's Dream: To have fun and see where that gets us! And although we haven't yet performed in public, we'll be at Amanda's garage all the time for practice!

Advice to Others: If you're thinking about starting a band, you've gotta love your instrument. Otherwise music becomes a chore. You also have to choose people you get along with really well.

CHAPTER SEVEN

Will We Ever Sound
Like Rock Stars?

Some people think "practice" and "rehearsal" are the same thing. No way! *Practice* is what you do on your own to become better on your individual instrument. *Rehearsal* is when your whole band gets together to work on your sound and your performance as a group. Practice and rehearsal are two of the most important steps in your ladder to the top.

Where Can We Make Some Noise?

Where can you practice and rehearse? If you have one of those quieter instruments—an acoustic guitar or piano—your house will probably work fine for practicing. Drums and electric instruments may be a little more of a noise problem for your family. If someone in your band has a garage and understanding parents, you're all set. But if not, there are lots of other places where you might find room.

The best thing is to find a ready-made practice room that you can use in exchange for occasional performances. Maybe your band would agree to play for the school assembly in exchange for a chance to practice in the school auditorium when the janitors are cleaning after school. If you offer to play for a PTA fund-raiser, they might help you find a room. Ask your local YMCA or Goodwill—maybe you can trade volunteer work for rehearsal space. If there is a dance studio close by, your band may be able to rehearse at odd hours and then play for the dancers in exchange. Also, don't forget to check with your network.

Soundproofing

Often it's necessary to do some soundproofing to keep your noise level down. The bass and drums are usually what bother the neighbors and they are the hardest instruments to play quietly. An inexpensive way to quiet down is to cover the walls with old carpet or blankets. Hang them from the ceiling to the floor, leaving a gap of air space between the carpet and the wall. You can also hot glue large egg crates to the carpets for extra soundproofing. Check with your network, because they'll know about new products and other tips for solving your soundproofing problem.

Practice Makes Perfect

Practice is the kind of work you do alone, away from everyone else. Whether in a garage or your bedroom, you should practice every day. Get yourself a metronome, a small drum machine, or anything that will give you a steady beat, and practice to the rhythm. This is a time for you to master your scales and techniques, a time to fall in love with your music, and a time to experiment (*after* you've practiced the basics).

Music is a lot like sports—not everyone is willing to make the effort and sacrifices needed to make the team. For those who do, it's worth the work. Spend time practicing the things that give you the most trouble. Keep track of what you need to work on, then warm up to the hard stuff by playing the stuff you can handle. Take your time during practice and enjoy yourself. Don't rush to finish. This is your time to become a master.

Stay Motivated

When you practice by yourself, you need to keep up your motivation. Nobody's looking over your shoulder—you have to do it for yourself. If you find you can't concentrate, put your instrument down until you can. Do something else for a while, but come back to it after the break.

Real Rehearsals

Rehearsals should happen on a regular schedule, just like your personal practice time. There is a temptation at rehearsals to spend your time blabbing, messing around, and just having fun with your friends. You can find a balance between the work and play, but it's easy to spend your precious rehearsal time jamming strange chords for an hour, then chatting for a while, until your drummer needs to get home and soon your session is gone and no real work has been done.

Rehearsing is work, at least if you do it correctly, and *somebody* needs to take charge to make sure the work happens. Rehearsals should also be fun—especially after you master some songs and can start experimenting. But don't try jamming first . . . it's too easy to lose track of time and forget to rehearse the songs you *need* to learn.

Are you the born leader? As a group, your band needs to choose someone to keep the focus, just like the coach of a team. Sometimes the best leader for the band is the person who is the best listener. Everyone needs a person they can share the good and bad times with, someone to go to for advice or just to vent some steam. A good band leader is good at listening *and* keeping the band focused on making music.

If your band isn't making any progress at a rehearsal, agree to meet another night. Then you can go do something useful, like practicing on your own. Your band won't be able to focus every single time you rehearse, but if you put in the effort and insist on high-quality rehearsals, you'll be rewarded in the end. You will soon start sounding like rock stars!

Be Prepared

You wouldn't *dream* of showing up for basketball practice late, without your shoes, and so out of shape that you can't keep up with the rest of the team. The same goes for your band—everybody should come to rehearsal prepared for the session. They should bring examples of the songs they want to play, so you can decide together what will go on your song list. Once you decide which songs to learn, each musician should have his or her own parts ready for those songs when they come to rehearsal. It's important that everyone brings a good attitude. That will make it possible to accomplish what you planned.

All band members should stay on top of their homework, too, so there aren't any surprises when it comes time to perform. It's hard to play a gig when your bass player gets grounded for bad grades!

Keep It to Yourselves

Here's a very helpful tip: Keep your rehearsals PRIVATE! People don't need to know where or when you're going to do it, because you don't need any distractions. Of course boyfriends and girlfriends want to come and listen, but they are *no* help. So tell them no! No parents . . . no friends . . . no one who isn't in the band. No exceptions. You won't get anything done, you'll have no room to move, you'll have people talking and laughing in the middle of what was supposed to be rehearsal. What a mess! Your three-hour rehearsal will quickly dwindle to ten minutes of actual playing. You'll never make it at that pace.

Mirror, Mirror on the Wall . . .

Do you have a big mirror? Can you move it so you can watch yourselves while you rehearse? Is there a dance studio where you can arrange to have rehearsals? Watching yourself perform is good inspiration to keep you working hard.

In the same way, recording your music on tape will help you hear what you need to work on. You don't need an expensive recording outfit to do this; a decent tape recorder will do. Just be sure to use the same setup all the time so you can hear your progress as you improve. It's weird to hear and watch yourselves at first, but stick with it and work to become better. Someday you'll sound and look like a great band.

What Kinds of Songs Should We Practice?

Talk together about what you hear on tape, so you can make decisions about which songs work with your instruments and vocals and which you should throw out. What kinds of songs should you play? Of course you should play what you love, but keep in mind:

ROCK STAR SECRET #4:

When you are playing live, your balance of fast songs
to slow songs should be four fast songs
for every one slow song.

Your audience will be more likely to dance, or at least stick around for another song, with faster music.

Also, songs your audience already knows will keep them interested. You may want to cover a few well-known songs by famous bands, mixed in with your own to hold your audience's attention.

But don't just copy a song—make it your own. You can do very cool covers like the Fugees' "Killing Me Softly" or Cake's "I Will Survive," which are based on old songs but sound totally unique and new.

The Search for Perfection

At some point you will need some advice from someone who knows what they are talking about. You will need a teacher who can push you to improve, or you will need to talk to bands who are more experienced. Another great way to keep growing is by taking music seminars and workshops at your local music store or community college.

A unique opportunity to improve is **Soundwall Music Camp**, which is the only camp in the country especially for young rock musicians. The nonprofit camp, based in the San Francisco Bay area, lasts for a week in the summer. Young musicians from across the country meet and share their love for music. In the morning they attend classes on various types of rock: funk, blues, ska, hard rock, swing, etc. Then they get together and form "bands" that jam together. In the afternoon there are classes on theory and technique, and at night there are seminars on topics such as how to make it in the music business, voice, and stage technique. Teens also attend performances by guest musicians and form bands together to play in a concert at the end of the week! For more information check out the Web site www.rockcamp.org or tel/fax 925-831-8676 or write to 179 Oak Road, Alamo, CA 94507.

Cassandra Spangler

Drummer Extraordinare

About Cassandra: Cassandra Spangler is 16 years old, and she has played the drums for six years. Although she is still searching for the perfect band, she is dedicated to her instrument. She has also played the guitar for one year.

History: Cassandra loves being a drummer. She started at the age of 10 and knew right away that the drums were for her. Currently she practices every day: 30 minutes on exercises from her teacher, 30 minutes on technical skills, and 20 minutes on exercises to strengthen her arms, wrists, and ankles. She has been in a number of bands, but right now she is on the lookout for a new one. In the meantime she has played the drums for her school's honor band and is now focused on perfecting her technique. Cassandra has performed at school talent shows and at a battle of the bands.

My Greatest Experience: Attending Soundwall Music Camp, the only camp in the country for young musicians. At camp I gained experience playing many types of music, met cool teen musicians from across the country, and attended seminars on how to make it in the music business. For an entire week I was able to eat, sleep, and breathe music! I met a group of people who understand

C ASSANDRA S PANGLER

how important music is to me because it is just as important to them. (For more information on Soundwall, see page 66).

Worst Experience: In sixth grade each student who wanted to be in band had to have an interview with the band teacher. When I told him I wanted to play drums, he said I would be "better suited" to play the clarinet since I am a girl! Instead of letting him discourage me, I played clarinet in the band and took private drum lessons. The next year I changed schools and became the drummer in my new school's honor band. In some respects, this experience was actually positive because it taught me to rise above discrimination and use it to make me stronger rather than letting it discourage me.

Dream: To be in a talented punk band and use my influence to hold benefit concerts and bring music into the lives of inner-city kids. I would also like to own a record company and allow creative bands to gain exposure but still retain artistic control of their work.

Advice to Others: Never give up. A lot of people will try to dissuade you, but don't allow them to make you lose sight of your goals. Be involved in everything you can and be open to unusual opportunities.

CASSANDRA SPANGLER

ANDRÉS   ELISABETH   SHANE

Morboenia

Band Members: This band is an incredible mix of many different inspirations. They combine metal, classical, punk, and folk music from around the world for a sound that is truly unique. The band includes **Elisabeth Williams** (age 14) on lead vocals and guitar, **Shane Stylianos** (age 16) on drums, and **Andrés Wilson** (age 15) on lead guitar. To their music fans, these teens are known as Super Andrés, Shane, and Dead Stars.

The Band: Elisabeth and Andrés have been jamming together for a long time. For a while they wanted to start a band, but couldn't find a drummer who fit. Finally they met up with Shane (who responded to signs they posted) and Morboenia (mor-BAY-nee-ah) was formed! Since then they have had lots of local success playing at record stores and battles of the bands. They also get the opportunity to play concerts at their school. In the near future they will have the chance to be the opening band for concerts in Boston! These will be their first paid gigs, and they can't wait.

Our Greatest Experience: Once a local record store held a party and we were one of the bands invited to play, even though all the other bands were local adult bands! We gave a great performance to a very appreciative audience.

Worst Experience: One gig we were really excited about. We put posters everywhere and had everything set up, but no one came. We finally figured out that it had been announced at our school as a different day! It was sad, but we didn't give up.

Band's Dream: Fame would be nice, but we also enjoy being a popular local band. Our dream is to keep having a great time with our music wherever that takes us.

Advice to Others: Be original! We have become well-known locally because we are really different. Don't be afraid to try new stuff and use creativity liberally.

CHAPTER EIGHT

Finding Your Name, Look, Sound, and Songs

So, you've got your band. You're really getting into the practices and rehearsals. Things are going great. Then somebody asks you, *"What do you call yourselves?"* Oh yeah—your band needs a name. And not only a name, you need an identity. *Who are you?* What kind of music do you play? What are you all about? It's time to figure all this out.

What's in a Name?

Choosing a name for your band isn't as difficult as it might seem. Sometimes the best name is simply the one that you can all agree on. It might be one that comes easiest, or you might need to try out a few to see how they feel. Do some brainstorming for a bunch of possible names, then use these tips for choosing the right one:

• Poll your friends outside the band to see which name they like best.

• Your name should give people a clue about the kind of music you play. Does that give you any ideas?

• Sometimes it's cool to combine several names. Write each name idea on a piece of paper and put them in a sack. Draw a few and see if any of the bizarre combinations grab you.

• Look through books of poetry, the dictionary, thesaurus, your favorite comic book—anything that has words or ideas.

• Sleep on it. Great ideas often come in dreams.

Don't be afraid to change your band's name if you come up with a better idea. Lots of great bands started out with names that weren't so great. For instance, did you know that the Beatles were originally called the Quarrymen? It's hard to believe, but Jon Bon Jovi was once in a band called The Fat Pet Clams from Outer Space. I am *sure* that you can come up with a better name than that! Does it seem like all the good names are taken? Just remember to have fun with it. Play around with this part of your band's development. No matter what you end up calling yourselves, you'll have some good laughs.

Once you have your name, you can develop your band's logo. Can someone in your band design it? Do you have any friends in art class? Your logo should be a symbol that represents who you are. You can put it on business cards, T-shirts, posters, your bass drum head, and your backdrop. Never put your logo on a car or on the door to your practice room—that is just inviting people to steal your great equipment.

Looking Like the Band You Are

Back in the old days, bands had to wear matching outfits to be cool! Aren't you glad you're making music *now?* These days you can wear whatever you want. What an improvement! But your look, like your name, should reflect who you are—hard rock, country, rap, hip-hop, or something totally new. No matter what look you choose, you'll be happy if you follow some simple rules:

- Pick clothes that are comfortable, washable, and not too hot.
- Check out your local thrift stores to find your look for less money.
- Obviously you should show up to your gigs showered and fresh.

Set aside some of your rehearsal time to talk about your look. Make sure you're all on the same page when it comes to your stage look. This is more important than some bands realize. You want your audience to remember your band and your music, so wear clothes that tell them who you are.

Creating Your Sound

"Have you heard that great new band?" Will the kids in the hall be saying that about you? *No way,* you might be thinking, *we don't sound unique enough.* That's OK. Every successful band has a unique sound that takes time to develop. Sometimes it happens by accident and sometimes it's planned from the start. Don't wait for the accident; develop a plan as a band to create your special sound—the sound that sets you apart from other bands.

Of course you'll start out copying your favorite music. But if you want to become real rock stars, your band needs to emphasize your greatest unique strengths. Maybe you have a fabulous lead singer, so you'll concentrate on cool vocals with lots of harmonies. Or maybe your guitar player is the next Jimi Hendrix, so your songs focus on her solos. Perhaps everyone in your band plays several instruments, so your audience will have fun watching you mix and match, never sure what's going to happen next.

You may start out copying bands you admire, but as your band plays together more and more, you'll start to find your own voice and vision. It takes time and dedication, so stay focused until you find it. As you listen to other bands you admire, think about what is unique about their sound. What do you love about their music? Often your sound will form from bits and pieces of all the other bands that inspire you.

Writing Your Own Songs

ROCK STAR SECRET #5:

Most of the money made in music
comes from writing songs.

It's true! Every time your song is played on the radio, you receive royalty payments. The royalties from songwriting can last a lifetime. So this needs to be where you invest a lot of your talent. The great thing about songwriting is that anyone can write a song. This is your chance to show the world how unique you are. Here are some tips to get your ideas flowing:

- What makes you unusual? Has something happened in your life that changed who you are? Something great . . . or something terrible?

- Has something happened to someone you know? Lots of songs are written about someone else's experience.

- Check out your family history. Maybe your grandparents had crazy lives that would make a cool song.

- Have you ever been in love (or can you pretend)? There is always room for another good love song.

- Are you studying history in school? There are lots of interesting stories that haven't been told. You can bring a modern twist to an old subject.

- Do you have a hero? Can you think of someone who inspires you? Try writing a song about him or her.

- Pay attention to your dreams! They can often be the inspiration for wonderful and quirky songs. "Yesterday" came to Paul McCartney of the Beatles in a dream.

- Is creative writing offered at your school? That's a whole class for thinking up song ideas.

- How about poetry in English class? Lyrics are poetry!

- Pick up a newspaper. What's going on in the world? Anything that makes you really angry or happy? That's perfect for a song! For instance, U2's song "Sunday Bloody Sunday" was written about a massacre in Ireland.

- Keep a notebook handy just for song ideas that come to you. Soon it will become second nature to write them down. Paul McCartney of the Beatles had to write "Michelle" on a napkin because he wasn't prepared when the idea hit him.

- Keep a journal. It's a good place to look for ideas. And when you get famous you can also use your journal to write your best-selling autobiography!
- Any class can spark ideas, even science or math. So pay attention.
- So, you're bored. Hey, some great songs have been written when people were bored. Did you know Elvis's song "All Shook Up" was written about a can of Coke?
- Check with your network to find out about local songwriting groups that you can join. Keep your eye on bulletin boards in music shops and bookstores.

If you're open to the world around you, the song possibilities are endless! Most books about songwriting (listed in Chapter 15) give you creative exercises to do. If you do them, you'll never run out of song ideas. You'll be surprised at how much you have to write about already!

ALLISON   SARAH   TERRI

The Hurricane Girls

An Up-and-Coming Band

Band Members: These girls may be young, but they are definitely dedicated to their music! The Hurricane Girls are three vocalists from Wisconsin who sing pop to pre-recorded music. They are: **Sarah Mandley** (age 9), **Allison Mandley** (age 11), and **Terri Quappé** (age 11).

The Band: Although this band is just starting out, they are clearly talented and headed for great things. They have all been involved in music for quite a while and they finally decided to put it all together. After they had written several songs, The Hurricane Girls took their music to a recording studio. They loved singing into the mike and listening to the playback. They now send their demo tape out for contests and performing opportunities. Recently they were chosen to play at their school talent show. Keep up the great work, Hurricanes!

Our Greatest Experience: When we wrote our first song together, "The Power of a Smile." We worked out the lyrics, developed the harmony, and were so excited to realize we could write beautiful songs.

Band's Dream: To have fun performing our music for others.

Advice to Others: Work hard, but remember to have fun with your music.

CHAPTER NINE

Will Anyone Come See Us?

PERFORMING AND GETTING GIGS

My voice is an ordinary voice. What people come to see is how I use it.

— Elvis

Stage Fright

Does the idea of going on stage, in front of thousands of people, with all the lights on you, make you a little nervous? If so, you're not alone. Some people are naturally comfortable in front of a crowd, but most of us need experience before we overcome our fears. Whether you're already cool with it or not, the more time you spend on stage performing for people—in music, theater, public speaking, even dance—the better you're going to be when it's your band's turn in the spotlight.

Every time you play your music, imagine yourself on stage. Maybe you're just playing for a few friends after school (so it's a small stage) but that's how you learn to put on a real show. All you need now is experience playing in front of *more* people. The more you perform, the sooner you'll become comfortable with it and the faster success will find you.

Do Some Spying

Make time as a band to go see other bands play. Do your performing "homework" together and listen to as many bands as you can. Watch and listen to how they keep time, how they dress, etc. Make notes about the things they do that you and the audience like— things you can incorporate into your performances, as well as things to avoid.

What do other bands do *between* songs? Nothing is more annoying to fans than waiting while bands endlessly mess with their instruments. This should be *absolutely prohibited!* A good band keeps their fans entertained between songs—chatting with the audience, explaining the next song, making jokes, announcing upcoming performances or CD releases.

ROCK STAR SECRET #6:

Your attitude toward your fans is just as important as your musical talent.

Never forget that you're entertaining your fans, and they want to *relate* to you. If you're outgoing, friendly, and genuine, they'll tell everybody how great you are. If you're rude, conceited jerks, what do you think they'll say? Every time you lose a fan, you also lose most of their friends! Gaining back lost fans is tough. Keeping them happy is a lot easier.

Get Down

What about dancing? Not only is dancing to your music fun, but it will improve your stage performance. Have you ever seen a band whose feet seem to nailed to the floor? They look like uncomfortable amateurs! If a band can play, but can't move to their own music, they seem stiff and boring. You, on the other hand, want to be a rock star! When your fans come to see you, you want them to experience an unforgettable, kickin' show. If you can dance to your music, you can get your audience to dance to it, too. Then *everybody's* having a great time. Giving a dance-worthy show gives you another advantage over other bands. It might even be worthwhile to take a few dance lessons if you've got two left feet—whatever it takes to *get down*.

In the Beginning . . .

As soon as your band learns some songs, get out there and play them in front of others. How many songs do you need? Six songs can be enough for a good start, and up to fifteen would be even better. Whatever number you decide on as a band, *keep the songs simple and play them well.*

Stay in your "comfort zone" while you're learning to play in front of a crowd. Don't try to do too much too soon or you'll freak yourselves out. And *don't* worry about making money at the start. If you need to make money, make it working at something else. At the beginning, you don't want the pressure of *having* to make money with your music. Just try to get comfortable and enjoy your music for a while.

All the World's a Stage

How many opportunities can you find to perform? You can start with family events (birthdays, weddings, etc.) and expand your horizons as you gain confidence. Is there a community or church choir where you live? The Backstreet Boys got their start singing in the church choir. Can you join a theater? Does your school have classes in music or drama? Even a speech class or debate club would help your stage presence. Be open to any and all possibilities for performing in front of people. Your local chamber of commerce may have a list of events, clubs, and organizations that are looking for entertainment.

Getting Gigs

Gigs are great! If you're willing to volunteer your band to raise money for worthy causes, you will have no problem finding great places to play. If you are playing for free, it's perfectly acceptable to ask for *some* kind of compensation—food for the band, transportation to and from the gig, a sound system and a technician to run it, or free publicity.

Get that first gig out of the way as soon as you can. Play a party for friends or family or play at an open mike event at a nearby coffeehouse. If you are nervous, practice looking above the audience's heads. If you don't *act* nervous, they will never know. Also, never react when you make a mistake—you will probably be the only one who notices. Once you play your first gig, you can relax and work on improving your show.

Play for free until you feel confident that you have enough material and stage experience that fans will *pay* to see you. Then you can start charging. Don't expect to earn much money at first. When you are first starting to get paid, ask the event sponsor what the budget is, and be flexible. If you're uncomfortable setting a price, you might ask your network what a fair cover charge is. Eventually, when you have a following, you can plan on receiving around $100 to split between the band members for every gig you play.

Remember to be clear about what style of music you play. Don't promise something you can't do just to get the gig. Where are some good places to find gigs when you're starting out? Here are some ideas to get you going:

• School dances are where many bands start playing in front of crowds.

• Your school talent show can be a great place to get noticed by peers.

• How about your local mall or supermarket when they're having some special promotion? You could play for the new grand opening.

• Churches and synagogues are always looking for entertainment for their younger members.

• Hospitals are full of people looking for entertainment.

• Retirement homes usually appreciate young people who are willing to share their talents.

• County and state fairs always have entertainment and are great places to get discovered.

• Do some creative brainstorming! Don't forget about corporate parties, bar mitzvahs, fund-raisers, birthday parties, church socials, country clubs, weddings, theme parks, resorts, malls, hotels, art festivals, centennials, and anniversaries.

• Your local chamber of commerce will have a list of all the clubs and organizations in your area. They will also have a list of events going on in your town. All these events and organizations are going to need entertainment and help with fund-raising! Give them a call and volunteer your services.

• Your music network can help you learn about your local music scene. They can tell you which clubs are looking for new bands and who will pay the best.

Hanson was discovered by a representative from Mercury Records who came to see them at the state fair in their hometown of Tulsa, Oklahoma. Elvis won second place in a talent contest at a county fair in Tupelo, Mississippi. N'Sync were playing in coffeehouses and theme parks when they got their first recording contract. Look around your community and pay attention to where people gather for any occasion. Do they need music? Of course! So, that's where you start. First your hometown, then the world!

Grow a Thick Skin

A final word of wisdom on performing: *Toughen up!* You definitely need a thick skin to be in the music business. There are always going to be people who don't like your music, your look, your name, or your drummer's hair color. Everyone has an opinion—the concert promoters, music critics, audiences, and even your parents! Keep in mind that sometimes people will criticize you because they'd like to be able to do what you do, but they can't or they're too afraid to try. They may criticize you just because they're jealous! Learn to let their comments roll off you. They are just opinions, not necessarily the truth. Take what's helpful to you—any advice that might make you a better band—and ignore the rest.

SHAWN   MIKE   JONATHAN
DRUMS: ROBERT

The Otherworld

Band Members: This progressive rock and alternative band has five great members: **Jonathan Nistal** (age 17) plays guitar, **Robert Moran** (age 17) plays drums, **Mike Moran** (age 13) plays guitar, **Shawn Beattie** (age 17) plays bass, and **Bill Fitzpatrick** (age 18) plays keyboard.

The Band: The Otherworld has been jamming together for 2 ½ years. They are made up of five excellent musicians; their drummer has been playing for 8 years. Together they have played gigs at bowling alleys, block parties, and several talent shows. One of their greatest honors was being chosen, along with two other bands, to play at a benefit in Christopher Morley Park for Students Against Drunk Driving. Right now they are concentrating their efforts on songwriting. They have three incredible original songs, with six more in the works. They are focused on finishing these songs so they will have enough material for an album.

Greatest Experience: One block party we played where everyone loved our music. Basically anytime you put us on a stage, we never want to get off.

Worst Experience: One gig that got cancelled. We hate to miss a chance to play!

Band's Dream: To send a professionally recorded demo tape to a record company and have them love it.

Advice to Others: Find other musicians who you can really work with. It does take time and effort, but eventually you will grow as a band.

MATTHEW   ANDREW   MARC

P.D.T. Band

Band Members: This band is made up of two brothers who have been jamming together practically since birth. They started out on Sesame Street banjos and drums! They have since upgraded their instruments and now they have been joined by another talented musician. Together, they play a mixture of rock and blues. The band includes **Andrew Sutin** (age 12), who has played the drums for five years, **Matthew Sutin** (age 14), who has played the guitar for four years, and **Marc Calderaro** (age 14), a talented bass player.

The Band: The members of this dedicated band practice 90 minutes each day on their own, and then four hours each week together. Their dedication has brought them several paid gigs. They have played for birthday parties, town fairs, and libraries, and they do a gig every other Friday night for a local coffeehouse. They also play for the South Jersey Junior Pops Orchestra. The five-year-old Sutin brother looks forward to joining the band someday and has already begun learning the violin!

A great moment for the band was when they met a local recording producer through their music teacher. Since then they have started working together to record and mix their music. Soon they will have cassettes to sell at their gigs.

P . D . T . B A N D

Our Worst Experience: Our worst and greatest experiences are actually related. About a week before we played at Westampton Day, we lost the bass player who had agreed to play with us! We were in a state of shock.

Greatest Experience: The same night we lost our bass player there was a local band playing at our library. We went and met them and told them about our problem. The lead guitarist offered to play bass for us! Playing with him at Westampton Day was our greatest experience!

Band's Dream: To be popular musicians, to do our best, make money from our music, and have fun.

Advice to Others: Practice, have fun, and believe in your dreams! It is easy to find gigs if you are willing to do them as a benefit to your community. This will get your music heard and may lead to paid gigs. Be involved with your local music scene and become friends with other musicians. You can help each other out by recommending each other or passing gigs to each other that you are unable to keep yourself.

P. D. T. BAND

CHAPTER TEN

Doing Demos, Attracting Attention, and Getting Discovered

The time will come when you're ready to try for the top. Then what? While you're looking for your "break," remember that your break is looking for you, too! There are tons of music reps searching the country for the next hot band. Could it be you? Of course! But don't just sit around waiting for the big break to find you. Make it easy for them. There are some things you can do that will radically increase your chances of getting discovered.

Do We Do a Demo?

Once your band has a name, a look, a sound, and performing experience, you may decide it's time to make a *demo*. A demo is a high-quality tape of your band playing that you send out to promote yourselves. You'll be sending it to possible gigs, to record companies, to agents, etc. You may also want to make a videotape of yourselves so you can show people how you perform.

Protecting Your Art

The first step in making a demo is copyrighting your original songs. This protects you from someone else stealing your material and getting rich and famous off your brilliance. To copyright songs, write a letter to the Register of Copyrights, Library of Congress, Washington, DC 20559; ask them for music copyright forms. When you get the paperwork, register your songs as a collection—it's the cheapest way to go. You might also ask someone to check the forms for accuracy. Once you have your copyright, you can let people know that your music is protected by writing or typing the copyright symbol, the year you copyrighted it, and your name. For instance, if Jean Rock wrote a song in 1999, she would make sure her demo tape had a label that said: copyright © 1999 by Jean Rock.

Recording Your Songs

There is a huge variation in a demo's quality and price. At the high end you can go to a professional recording studio, which can be very expensive. At the low end you can use your own tape recorder in your kitchen, which will give you reverb. If you can't spend any money, that is exactly what you should do. The secret is to use a better microphone than the one that comes built into your tape recorder. Almost any mike is better, and the quality of the mike makes a big difference. The sooner you can record your own songs the better. You probably won't like your first efforts—it's a little shocking the first time you hear yourself! Stick with it, though, and add better equipment as you can afford it.

The next step up in quality and price is a four-track tape recorder that you can work at home. *Four-track* means that each instrument you use can be on a different track. For example, on track one you record the guitar, on track two you record the drums, on three you have vocals, and on four you have bass. The tracks are all synchronized and you can alter the volume of each track so that the lead instrument or vocal can be louder. You must have good mikes for good results, and the acoustics of the room you use will affect the sound. For more ideas, check out the book called *The Musician's Guide to Making and Selling Your Own CDs and Cassettes*, listed in Chapter 15.

The highest jump in quality and price is the professional recording studio. They usually have 64 tracks! This is probably more than you need, but you would be surprised at how many tracks they use to create the songs you hear on the radio. The results they produce are worth the investment, and you might get lucky and find a studio producer who believes in you and your music. (That's what happened to the Beatles.)

Making a demo can be pretty expensive, so check with your network about the best place to make a demo. It's likely they'll know the cheapest studio in your area. When you choose a place, try bargaining with them. Could they use some help labeling their millions of audio and videotapes? Maybe they'd trade you services, or at least give you a discount on your demo.

If you don't have the money to pay for a professional studio, there are other options. Get in touch with any techno friends you have. You need a tape of your songs and a videotape of your band. *They* have the equipment and love to experiment. Make a deal. How would they like your band to play for their party? Also, lots of schools have recording and video equipment. If you can take classes in sound and video production, or at least get to know the teens and teachers in those programs, you'll be able to create some good demo tapes for very little cash.

Duplications

Once you have a good recording of your band, there are companies that will create CDs or tapes from your master. You can use these tapes and CDs to promote yourselves, or you can sell them at gigs. Many bands make a good profit by doing this. Alanis Morissette recorded her own demo and then sold copies on the bus! One place that makes cassettes and CDs from your original recording is Kaba Audio. They work with people with all levels of experience, from all over the country, and they are pretty affordable, too. You can call them at 1-800-231-8273 or write to them at 24 Commercial Blvd., Suite E, Novato, CA 94949.

A Word About Publicity

Getting the word out about your band is really important! When you have gigs, put signs or posters around your community. When you win an award or have a special performance, call your local newspaper and see if they will cover the story. And don't forget about national media! Many music magazines love featuring young, hip bands. Send pictures and information about yourself. You can send this to music magazines and other teen magazines like *Jump*, *Time for Kids*, *Girl's Life*, etc. If you work at getting publicity, eventually word will get around and you will have a following.

Grab Their Attention

"NXNW" . . . "SXSW" . . . What are those—Russian street names? No, they stand for "North by Northwest" and "South by Southwest"—music events held in Portland, Oregon, and in Austin, Texas, where hundreds of bands play mostly for free so they can be seen by lots of record company scouts. These festivals, and others like them, are always looking for good new bands to sign up. Check your newspaper and your network to see what festivals or talent searches are going on near you. State and county fairs are also a great place to get discovered.

You'll need that demo to send to these and other events. But don't rush it. Make sure you're a good *live* band first! Some bands sound great on their demo, but out on stage they bomb! If you get discovered and signed to a label, they'll want you to go out on tour to promote your CD. If you can't play live, you won't be famous for long.

Once you have your demo, send it to the record companies that handle bands playing your kind of music. In other words, if you play heavy metal, don't send your demo to the New Age company that makes Yanni's CDs! You'll find the addresses for all the record companies in *The Music Address Book* (see Chapter 15). If you think your favorite musician might be interested in a song you wrote, you can find his or her address in there, too. By all means, send them a copy of your tune (*after* you copyright it, of course!). Musicians are always on the look-out for good material. Many great rock stars, such as Sheryl Crow, began their careers by writing music for other artists.

Once you have fans and lots of experience, you may want to incorporate a lighting system. Good lighting enhances the mood throughout your performance and helps people get into your music. You can start out with a few red and blue spotlights that you can turn on and off from the stage. Your local music network can tell you where to find them. Your school, university, or community theater can teach you a lot about lighting and stage work. Volunteer for production assistance and get to know the people who do the technical performance. Although this kind of equipment is expensive, it adds a lot to your show.

Can We Manage Without a Manager?

At some point you'll probably need a manager—someone who knows the music industry and gets paid by how successful you become. Usually you need a manager when the financial part of your career starts taking up more time than the music part. Back to your network . . . your trusted advisors know who can help you, or at least where to look. Any agreements you make should be short-term. That way you have a chance to test them out. If they're lousy, you won't have to wait for years to get rid of them.

Lately, the trend for a lot of bands has been to go to the "Indies" instead of getting a manager. The Indies are small, independent record companies that promote bands on a smaller scale than the huge companies. They don't have the same kind of money to promote bands like the big outfits, but they concentrate more of their efforts on you. They may give you a chance when major record labels won't even listen to your demo! They often create a big buzz for an unknown band, which then makes it to the top.

We've Been Discovered!

Are you good enough to be discovered? Then you can count on it happening! There are lots of books about what to do if it happens to you (see Chapter 15). Read a few so you're prepared for the hard stuff. But also remember to enjoy your success. You earned it!

BRITTANY   BRIANE

Twice

Band Members: This is a vocal group which sings *a cappella* or to their own pre-recorded music. They call their music *revival pop rock* because they take the old rock and pop sounds and change them to sound more like today. The band includes two talented sisters: **Brittany Sorice** (age 12) as soprano and **Briane Sorice** (age 15) who is alto/soprano.

The Band: Twice practices at least three times a week in their basement "studio." They have been performing together since they were little kids, but have had particular success in the last three years. Lately they have received many invitations to sing and have performed at about 20 private parties, as well as at local hospitals, nursing homes, and churches. You can often find them singing at school talent shows. They enjoy singing on the boardwalk, and one time a huge crowd gathered to listen. Although in public the girls only sing, they know a lot about music since they play the drums, guitar, piano, and recorder!

Our Greatest Experience: Our greatest experience was when we received an offer to make a demo CD from an independent record producer! We gave them the music chords and let them know how we wanted it done. Then they recorded the music and finally we went into the studio to record our voices.

Worst Experience: When we were starting out some people thought we were just little kids and they didn't take us seriously.

Band's Dream: To get our music out there and have a lot of fun with it all!

Advice to Others: Keep working at it, no matter what people say, and never give up! Whether you are singing, playing, or writing, put in everything you've got.

TWICE

CHAPTER ELEVEN

Will We Be Rich?

Give Us Money!

Making money from your music is so much fun! But it can also be a source of conflict within your band. It's a good idea to discuss the band's finances once a month so you all know where you stand. There usually isn't enough to go around at the beginning, so you need to decide how you are going to divide your earnings. Equal money for equal work is the best way. If everyone does their fair share of work, this method works well. If someone slacks off, it's best to talk directly to the person instead of talking behind his or her back. Perhaps your band can decide on some "slacker fines" to encourage everyone to do part of the work.

Save It for a Rainy Day

Early on, most bands take just a bit out of earnings to pay each band member; the rest goes into a band savings account that can be used to buy communal gear, pay for expenses, and cover emergencies. For example, if the bass amp breaks down, the bass player can borrow from your savings so the band can play the next gig. Often there are expenses involved with a gig. You'll need to take that money out of the band fund.

When your band has a name and an identity, start a bank account using your band name as an *assumed business name*. Decide who will be responsible for signing the band checks. Choose this person carefully—maybe a parent that you all respect, or the band member who is the most dependable, trustworthy, and reliable.

Dealing with Taxes

Check with your state's laws to see when you need to start paying taxes on your earnings. It's usually only after you each earn $1000 in a year. As a musician, you can deduct things from your taxes like money spent for travel, gear, and clothing. So, keep good records of what you spend—save all your receipts. It will save you a lot of money in the long run.

Watch Out for Sharks

The music business seems to have more than its share of sharks who prey on the inexperienced. The best way to make sure you get all the benefits of your hard work is to learn how to handle money yourself. This is one of the most important skills to learn in your music career. Once you start earning some real money, it would be great to find a friendly accountant or lawyer; or ask your parents for help. Your local musicians union will also have good financial information, plus a list of local music attorneys for specific questions. There are lots of good books, including *Music Law* (see Chapter 15), that will teach you what you need to know about the money side of music.

There's plenty of money to be made in music, but it can vanish overnight if you don't know what you're doing. Too many great musicians have lost it all because they couldn't handle their money. Don't let it happen to you! Learn all you can, and when the time comes, hire professionals for the stuff that takes you away from making your music.

Joanna Pisterzi

About Joanna: This experienced and talented soloist has been performing since she was 7 years old. Joanna is now 17 and her love for singing is as strong as ever. She sings classic ballads, blues, '70s songs, and contemporary Christian.

History: Joanna started out singing in musicals. She has played the lead in musicals such as *Bye Bye Birdie, A Christmas Carol, Heidi,* and *Annie.* She moved into solo work at the age of 11 when her sister asked her to sing for her wedding. After that performance, six other people scheduled her to perform at their wedding receptions and ceremonies. Now she practices voice two or three hours every day and can accompany herself on the piano or guitar.

Joanna realized that she wanted to sing forever when she performed in a talent show in front of 400 people on a cruise ship. She is a member of her school's top choir and has performed with them in Italy. Joanna is always looking for opportunities to sing—she even went to New York City for a talent contest. She met with agents and songwriters and learned about the business. But one of her greatest opportunities has been the State of Illinois solo/ensemble contest. She took second place four years ago, and has won first place for the past three years!

JOANNA PISTERZI

My Greatest Experience: Once I was performing just for fun at a karaoke restaurant. After I finished, a woman came up to me, gave me a hug, and told me that I was wonderful. She said that she would love to come to one of my concerts someday and asked for my autograph. Then she bought one of my demo tapes.

Dream: To make it big in music. I know it will be a challenge, but I am willing to work for it. I dream of performing at Chicago's New World Music Theatre.

Advice to Others: Stay focused—know what you want and work hard. Have fun and keep practicing.

JOANNA PISTERZI

CHAPTER TWELVE

Learning All the Skills You Need to Make It

You may be thinking, *Now I know everything I need to become a rock star.* What do I need school for? But in reality, there are a million reasons that school will help your music career. Surprisingly, *every* class will help you in some way—even if it just gives you ideas for quirky and unusual songs.

Love Your Library

Your school library should have some recordings of music that can give you musical ideas for your own songwriting. Many libraries offer Internet access, which is another great resource for you. Plus, librarians are known for their helpfulness and encouragement when they know what you need. So ask them!

Speak Your Mind

In speech and debate class you can learn to be a persuasive speaker. This will come in handy when you're a rock star—on stage, with MTV v-jays, and with magazine interviewers. You want to sound like a confident and well-spoken performer.

Act Out

You can learn to act, sing, and dance in your school's theater classes. As you know, these are the perfect skills to improve your stage presence. With theater experience, it will be easy for you to keep your fans entertained.

Calculate Your Success

As you know, learning how to handle your own money could save you a fortune when you become a rock star. A personal finance class will help you develop business skills so you'll know how to protect yourself from dishonest agents and managers. It will also teach you the money basics, such as how to open a bank account and write checks for your band.

Can You Compute?

What does a rock star need computers for? Learning about computers is actually one of the best things you can do for your music career. Everything from music programs to promotional materials to CD covers can be computer-generated.

The Internet is a great music world for you to explore. You can find out about other bands performing and get great info on what scouts are looking for. You could also set up your own band's Web site to handle fan mail!

MIDI is the future of music. MIDI stands for *Musical Instrument Digital Interface*; it is where most music recording and writing is happening now. It enables your instruments to "talk" to a computer, and then you can tell the computer exactly how you want the sound processed. So with MIDI you can play your guitar and have it sound exactly like a grand piano or a drum set! It allows one musician to become a full band or orchestra. MIDI controllers are built into most keyboards and are available for stringed instruments for around $200.

One Web site which is really helpful is www.mp3.com. They have a whole section where new artists can put their songs on the Web for fans to download. It is a great way to learn about new songs and get your songs well-known! They will even sell CDs for you if you have them.

Be Good to Your Body

A career in music is not for the weak and lazy! You need to keep yourself healthy and strong if you're going to look good, drag heavy equipment around, and keep up your energy to play late at night. Does your school have a good PE program? Can you lift weights at school? You don't want to end up a wimp from too many nights in the basement practicing your guitar. In fact, sports are a perfect training ground for aspiring rock stars. Playing a sport will help you stay in shape and make you a stronger competitor in your climb to the top of the music world.

After-School Activities

School clubs can teach you a lot about being a leader. You can pay attention to how leaders manage a group, and even try for those leadership positions yourself so you can learn the skills you need to run your own band.

What About College?

College may be your biggest chance to really make it big. Too many musicians drop their education to pursue music, only to regret it later when they have no other job skills. College isn't a stumbling block—it's actually an amazing opportunity. There are many cafes where bands can play and lots of college students who want to listen to the bands. There are also a lot of college events and parties that will want you to play for them. It's a great chance to get free exposure and to network with the future stars of the music industry. Plus, the more knowledgeable and articulate you are, the more respect you'll earn in the music world.

Some people think that musicians are uneducated, but that is not true at all. Did you know that Tori Amos was trained in classical piano from her very early childhood? Sheryl Crow has a university degree in classical piano, Elton John won a scholarship to the Royal Academy of Music in London, and Pat Benatar even studied opera! Would you have guessed that the lead singer of Rage Against The Machine graduated from Harvard? Monica was a serious student who finished high school with a 4.0 GPA and in spite of her fame she still plans to attend college.

Just about anywhere you look in school there are ways to increase your chances of becoming a rock star. Take advantage of every opportunity. And when your parents see your positive attitude toward school, you can bet they'll be big supporters of you and your dreams.

Sarah Carr

About Sarah: Sarah Carr is a vocal soloist. Although she is only 14 years old, she has been performing for four years. She enjoys singing rock, pop, and Christian music. She loves performing and feeling that so many people's hopes and dreams are brought out by her music.

History: Sarah has wanted to be a singer for as long as she can remember. She got her start by singing in her church. She has been the cantor solo (someone who sings the solo music for Mass) for four years. At the age of 12 she sang a solo at school for her school concert, and fell in love with the stage. Since then she has practiced every day and performed many times.

One of her greatest moments was when she was chosen as one of three people from her school to be in an interschool competition. At the competition she was awarded first place! The winners then went on to the city-wide meet, where Sarah placed seventh out of hundreds of vocalists!

My Greatest Experience: Winning first place in the school competition. I was sitting with my friends when the announcement came on. Third place was called, then second, and I thought that I hadn't won, but then they called my name for first place! I screamed and had tears in my eyes. All my friends were hugging me and congratulating me. It was great!

SARAH CARR

Worst Experience: One time I was singing at church and I was out of synch with the piano, so we had to start the song all over again. How embarrassing!

Dream: To make a difference in the way that music is played. I love performing and want to share my gift with the world.

Advice to Others: Stand out and be proud of yourself for what you can do and who you can be. I believe that with hope and belief in yourself, anyone can make it big.

SARAH CARR

NAVID   MATT   SKOT

Special Guests

Band Members: This popular band plays a combination of pop, rock, rap, and hip-hop. It includes three great musicians: **Navid Ghavamian** (age 16) plays bass guitar,

Matt Gervais (age 16) plays drums and backup vocals, and **Skot Suyama** (age 17) rocks on guitar and main vocals.

The Band: Special Guests is a band with a lot of great experience behind them. They have been playing together for over four years! During that time they have performed in many places, including charity benefit concerts, high school concerts, fashion shows, and assemblies. They have played at Seattle's University District Streetfair for the past three years, which is their favorite venue. They also won first place at their high school's battle of the bands.

Special Guests has recorded their music at several local recording studios. They now have great recordings which they use to promote themselves and to sell at their gigs.

Our Greatest Experience: One time Chris Cornell from Soundgarden was buying a motorcycle from Matt's neighbor! We didn't want to just walk up and ask for his autograph, so we opened the basement door, turned up

S P E C I A L   G U E S T S

the amps, and started playing one of his songs. Halfway through, Chris Cornell walked right into our jam room! He asked us to play one of our songs, thanked us, and gave us his autograph!

Worst Experience: The night before a big concert (the University Streetfair), Skot was singing the lead role in the high school musical. He sang his heart out and blew his voice! The next day 500 people showed up! Skot could hardly talk, much less sing. We played our best and apologized to the audience.

Band's Dream: To be famous and have an album out. Also that someone having a horrible day will listen to a song of ours and will feel better.

Advice to Others: Have fun with your music. If you can't be happy with the music you make and the gigs you get, then what is the point?

CHAPTER THIRTEEN

The Pitfalls of Fame

As we discussed earlier, your parents may not be too happy when you inform them, "Oh, by the way, I wanna be a rock star!" Can you imagine why? Well, aside from their terror about future hairdos, weird body piercings, headaches from 3 A.M. "jam sessions" in their basement, and nightmares of your dropping out of school to tour in

Albania, you can probably sum up the rest of their fears in two words: *drugs* and *alcohol.*

And guess what? Your parents are not insane. They're right to be concerned. Of course, you know better than to get caught up in that scene. But you're going to need all of your strength and integrity to keep resisting it. Why? Because drugs and alcohol are very common in the music business. The pressures you will face on your path to rock stardom will grow, and you need to be ready. Here are some tricks that will help you stay away from drugs and alcohol and stay true to your dreams.

Cigarettes

Nicotine is a deadly drug, as you well know. But it can be one of the easier ones for you to resist because cigarettes taste disgusting and are a huge waste of your hard-earned cash. Cigarettes will be offered to you a lot, but it's easy to say no without challenging the smoker to keep pressuring you. If you get tired of saying no all the time and feel uncomfortable saying you are too smart to do that stuff, say that you're allergic to nicotine (which is *true*, since everyone has a bad reaction to it at first). You can also claim to have asthma or a sore throat. Keep your reasons handy so you're not caught off guard and pressured into getting addicted to something that sucks up your needed cash and will kill you in the end!

Alcohol

Alcohol may be harder to resist, because you may perform at parties where alcohol is served. As you get older, you'll play gigs in clubs and bars where alcohol is all around you. It doesn't take long to get addicted. The easiest way out is not to drink it. When you are playing in places where alcohol is around, just keep a glass of your favorite juice or soda and politely refuse when alcohol is offered to you. Or tell people who pressure you, "No thanks, I'm the designated driver tonight."

Drugs

Other drugs out there are even worse for you—more expensive, more addictive, and more deadly. Drugs will ruin your body fast, and your career even faster. Some people think that when they take certain drugs they are able to make better music. The truth is that drugs make them totally out of touch with the real world, so they play forgettable, repetitive junk. Use the same kinds of excuses to say "no" . . . and then find some new friends and places to perform. Drugs are too dangerous to mess with. And besides, you have an *instrument* to learn!

If you decide to abuse alcohol and drugs, be aware that your career will be short. You can almost write your sad ending before you begin. Can you think of any other job in the world where you can use drugs and alcohol and be successful? No? That's because there aren't any. If you think you can do it as a rock star, you're crazy. The odds are against you.

Many brilliant musicians crush their dreams because they fall into addiction and lose their careers, their families, their friendships, and even their lives. Just look at the people who have tried it: Elvis, Janis Joplin, Kurt Cobain, Jimi Hendrix, and countless others were killed by their addictions. Give your dreams a chance and don't even get started. You'll have a much better chance of becoming a rock star if you're free of addictions . . . not to mention that you'll have a healthier, happier, and longer life!

LAURA   MEG   ADRI-ANNE

100% Cotton

Band Members: These girls are passionate about music and they want the world to know it. They play pop/gospel music mixed with a bit of rock and soul. The band includes: **Adri-Anne Ralph** (age 17) on bass and piano, **Laura Ralph** (age 15) on drums and piano, and **Meg Milner** (age 15) on drums and piano. Although the girls play instruments, their music revolves around their tight harmonies and vocal expertise.

The Band: Ever since this band formed in 1997, 100% Cotton has received invitations to perform. They started out playing as the worship team for their church, and have gone on to play at various schools, talent shows, and music festivals around Victoria, British Columbia. They were also invited to perform for the Totally Teen Talent show. Though over 250 groups auditioned, they were one of only 25 bands chosen! On the televised show, 15 performers were chosen for a final performance at a dinner theater, and again they made the cut. As a result of that performance they were chosen to be part of the upcoming Teen Coffeehouse gigs. Another chance to play came at MissionsFest, where they were one of three bands invited to play two years in a row. They have been involved in their local music scene and even co-produced the Victoria Young Artists' Showcase.

100% Cotton loved having the chance to record their music in a professional recording studio. They have had three sessions at the studio, and they recently made their first CD, which they sell at gigs.

100% Cotton

Our Greatest Experience: We attended a festival called Joyfest and during a break between scheduled performers we asked if we could go on. 100% Cotton sang three songs, and we were encored for two more! Afterwards we were approached by an independent record producer! It was a great feeling.

Worst Experience: One time we were excited for a big performance, but when we got there only eight people showed up and they weren't into our music at all.

Band's Dream: To make people happy and to have them walk out of our performances thinking, "I feel great!"

Advice to Others: Have integrity; always be true to your music and don't let anyone mold you into "what will sell." Don't be in it for the fame—love your music and be persistent.

1 0 0 % C O T T O N

CHAPTER FOURTEEN

You're On Your Way!

Now you understand the importance of practicing, rehearsing, and doing well in school. You need to develop *all* your skills if you want to be a rock star. You have to learn to speak and dance and sing and write . . . and even do math. It all helps your flight into a fabulous musical future.

You have a place to begin. You know how to get started, how to create your network to help you, and how to learn the skills you need. In this book you've met other teen bands with dreams like yours who are making it happen *right now*. And you can do it, too! Use what you've learned to reach your goal. If you put your imagination to work, you're capable of anything. Will you surprise everyone? Of course! Now you know how to realize your dream, so *go for it*!

GABRIELLE   MARGARET   JENNIFER   NICOLE   ERICA

Porcelain Dolls

An Up-and-Coming Band

Band Members: The Porcelain Dolls are an exciting pop and R&B band. They are made up of five 13-year-old girls who love to write their own music. The band includes: **Jennifer Parfidio, Margaret Lembo, Erica White, Nicole Iannitti,** and **Gabrielle Martin.** The Porcelain Dolls are an *a cappella* vocal band with a focus on complex, tight harmonies.

The Band: The Porcelain Dolls got together over a year ago and since then they have practiced diligently—it is beginning to pay off. They have had the opportunity to play for different events at school, such as plays and assemblies. They also played in a talent show where they received a standing ovation and won first place! These girls love the stage and never want to get off.

Our Greatest Experience: Our first time in a real recording studio. We learned the ins and outs of the music industry, and got the chance to record our music. It was anything but easy, but that just made us appreciate it even more. We would like to thank our vocal instructor, Brian Frame, for all his support.

Band's Dream: To influence others and never give up. Where we live there are not many teens to look up to, but we want to show that anything is possible.

Advice to Others: Unity! Stick together through thick and thin. We may not always agree, but it makes us work harder and appreciate each other's ideas more.

CHAPTER FIFTEEN

More Resources to Help You Become a Rock Star

BOOKS FOR ROCK STARS

Beginning Songwriter's Answer Book
by Paul Zollo; paperback; Writers Digest Books;
ISBN: 0898795613

The Songwriter's Idea Book: 40 Strategies to Excite Your Imagination, Help You Design Distinctive Songs, and Keep Your Creative Flow
by Sheila Davis; hardcover; Writers Digest Books; ISBN: 0898795192

Writing Better Lyrics
by Pat Pattison; hardcover; Writers Digest Books; ISBN: 0898796822

500 Songwriting Ideas: For Brave and Passionate People
by Lisa Aschmann; paperback; Mix Bookshelf/Mix Books; ISBN: 0918371155

The Songwriter's Musician's Guide to Making Great Demos
by Harvey Rachlin; paperback; Music Sales Corporation; ISBN: 0846426307

Protecting Your Songs and Yourself
by Kent J. Klavens; ISBN: 0898793645

The Music Business: Career Opportunities and Self-Defense
by Dick Weissman; Three Rivers Press; ISBN: 0517887843

The Music Business (Explained in Plain English): What Every Artist and Songwriter Should Know to Avoid Getting Ripped Off!
by David Naggar, Jeffrey D. Brandstetter (contributor), Scb Distributors; ISBN: 0964870908

With Your Own Two Hands: Self-Discovery Through Music
by Seymour Bernstein; paperback; Hal Leonard Publishing Corporation; ISBN: 0793557127

The Musician's Guide to Making and Selling Your Own CDs and Cassettes
by Jana Stanfield; paperback; Writers Digest Books; ISBN: 0898798086

Live Sound for Musicians
by Rudy Trubitt; paperback; Hal Leonard Publishing; ISBN: 0793568528

The Memory Book
by Harry Lorayne, Jerry Lucas; paperback; Ballantine Books (Trade Paperback); ISBN: 0345410025

The Sax and Brass Book
by Tony Bacon; Miller Freeman Books ISBN: 0879305312

Better Than a Lemonade Stand: Small Business Ideas for Kids
by Daryl Bernstein; Beyond Words Publishing; ISBN: 1885223153

Music Address Book
by Michael Levine ISBN: 0809591669
> The addresses of all your favorite rock stars.

Music Law: How to Run Your Band's Business
by Richard Stim ISBN: 087337438

MAGAZINES FOR ROCK STARS

Alternative Press

6516 Detroit Ave., Suite 5

Cleveland, OH 44102-3057

> A cool guide to alternative rock bands and music.

The Source: the Magazine of Hip-Hop Music, Culture & Politics

PO Box 1966

Marion, OH 43306-2066

> Gives a complete rundown of all new rap and R&B groups, plus great in-depth interviews.

Guitar World

1115 Broadway

New York, NY 10010

> Provides tons of information on guitars and rock bands and includes sheet music and lyrics at the back of the magazine.

Circus: America's Rock Magazine

6 West 18th Street

New York, NY 10011

> Offers personal glimpses into the lives of rock stars, and is filled with photos of your favorite alternative bands.

Spin Magazine

PO Box 51635

Boulder, CO 80322-1635

Rolling Stone

1290 Avenue of the Americas

New York, NY 10104-0298

URB: Future, Music, Culture

1680 N. Vine St., Suite 1012

Los Angeles, CA 90028

> A cool and diverse guide to R&B, rap, and alternative music.

Guitar Player

PO Box 58591

Boulder, CO 80322-8591

Acoustic Guitar

PO Box 767

San Anselmo, CA 94979-9938

The Performing Songwriter

6620 McCall Drive

Longmont, CO 80503

Musician: The Art, Business and Technology of Making Music

PO Box 1923

Marion, OH 43306-2023

www.musicianmag.com

The 1999 Musician's Guide to Touring and Promotion

Periodical; ISBN: 999209530X

This useful guide is updated yearly.

Piano and Keyboard Magazine

PO Box 2626

San Anselmo, CA 94979-2626

Note Service Music

Dept. GWA78

PO Box 4340

Miami, FL 33014

1-800-628-1528

A great source for videos and music for guitar.

Double Bassist

Orpheus Publications

PO Box 363

Avenel, NJ 07001

1-800-688-6247

ORGANIZATIONS FOR ROCK STARS

American Federation of Musicians

1501 Broadway

New York, NY 10036

American Music Scholarship Association

1030 Carew Tower

Cincinnati, OH 45202

International Piano Guild

PO Box 1807

Austin, TX 78767

International Society of Bassists

School of Music

Northwestern University

Evanston, IL 60208

WEB SITES FOR ROCK STARS ~ well (?)

www.unm.edu/~loritaf/pnoedmn.html

> The best piano Web site!

www.rockhall.com

> The rock Hall of Fame and museum.

www.eeb.ele.tue.nl/midi/index.html

> All about MIDI.

www.thesongwriter.com

> Has a great guitar songwriting guide.

www.und.nodak.edu/dept/mcr/

Music composition resource.

www.era.org.uk/

The copyright Web site for protecting your songs.

www.rolandcorp.com/

Leading maker of keyboards, guitar synthesizers, and techno gear.

www.alesis.com/

Affordable and dependable drum machines. Their reverb units are used everywhere.

www.fender.com/

Makers of great guitars and amplifiers.

www.mackie.com/

Reasonable sound system gear and great technical support.

www.mutual-music.com/

A free interactive music industry resource directory.

www.mp3.com/

A site where you can listen to other people's music and post your own on the Web as well. They will even sell CDs for you if you have them.

WANT TO EARN YOUR OWN MONEY?
LEARN HOW TO START A BUSINESS!

Learn fun ways to earn $$$ as a
- babysitting broker
- dog walker
- mural painter

and many, many more!!!

Fifteen-year-old Daryl Bernstein started his first
business when he was just eight years old. Since then he's tried all 51 of the
kid businesses in this book. Daryl now runs his own multi-million-dollar
business and is ready to share his secrets with you!

"Dear Daryl,

When I got Better Than a Lemonade Stand, *I came up with a great business idea
and earned enough money to buy a laptop computer! I never knew it would only take
one summer to earn the money. Thanks for your help."* —Brady, age 12

150 pages, black & white cartoon art, $8.95 softcover

WELL, EXCUUUUSE US!!!
HERE ARE ALL THE EXCUSES YOU'LL EVER NEED!

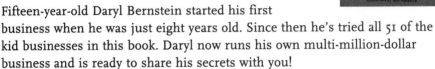

You'll get the best excuses for
- going to bed late
- not eating your vegetables
- not cleaning your room

and many, many more!!!

Mike and Zach are the excuse experts! At ages ten and
eleven, these best friends tested hundreds of excuses on family, friends, and
teachers in order to give you the best lines to get out of anything.

"Dear Mike and Zach,

*My whole class loves your book! I have an idea for excuses not to do your home-
work in the car: 'But Mom, it's homework, not carwork!'"* —Blakeney, age 10

96 pages, black & white cartoon art, $5.95 softcover

**For a free catalog or to order books,
call Beyond Words Publishing 1-800-284-9673**

HEY, GIRLS!!!
SPEAK OUT! BE HEARD!
BE CREATIVE! GO FOR YOUR DREAMS!

Discover how you can
- handle grouchy, just plain ornery adults
- pass notes in class without getting caught
- avoid life's most embarrassing moments
- unlock the writer inside you
and much, much more!!!

✷ A Scholastic Book Club Selection ✷

Girls Know Best celebrates your unique voices and wisdom. Thirty-eight girls, ages seven to fifteen, were picked to share their advice and activities with other girls. Everything you need to know . . . from the people who really know the answers—girls just like you!

160 pages, black & white collage art, $8.95 softcover

DO YOU HAVE A PSYCHIC PET?

Psychic Pets includes
- spooky stories of pets with psychic powers
- tests to find out if your pet is psychic
- tests to find out if you are psychic
- ways to increase your pet's psychic abilities
- astrology charts for your pet

✷ A Scholastic Book Club Selection ✷

Can your cat get out of the house even when all the doors are closed? Has your dog ever seen a ghost? Does your horse seem to read your mind? If you can answer yes to any of these questions, you might have a psychic pet!

"This amazing book is packed with incredible stories from all around the world, and there are fun psychic tests for you and your pet to do, too!" — Girl Talk magazine

124 pages, black & white art, $7.95 softcover

ARE YOU A GODDESS IN THE MAKING?

Meet thirty-six goddesses, including
- Athena, the Greek goddess of wisdom
- Tara, the Tibetan goddess of mercy
- Pele, the Hawaiian goddess of fire

and many, many more!

✳ A Book-of-the-Month Club Selection ✳

Gorgeous illustrations and fascinating stories
will introduce you to goddesses from many dif-
ferent cultures. See the beauty, power, and wisdom of these goddesses and
learn how they are still honored in countries around the world.

64 pages, color illustrations, $17.95 hardcover

DO YOU BELIEVE?

Check out the *Fairy Flora Guide* that tells you
the special plants and flowers that fairies love.
You can even attract fairies to your house by
planting your own magical fairy garden!

✳ A Book-of-the-Month Club Selection ✳

This book will introduce you to fairies, mer-
maids, pixies, and gnomes from around the
world. In this enchanting collection of stories
from France, China, England, India, Ireland,
Japan, and the Algonquian and Ojibwa tribes of America, fairies teach
humans the secrets of nature.

80 pages, color illustrations, $18.95 hardcover

**For a free catalog or to order books,
call Beyond Words Publishing 1-800-284-9673**

MORE ADVICE FROM GIRLS FOR GIRLS!

Learn how to:
- have the greatest slumber party of all time
- analyze your dreams
- handle life if your best friend ditches you
  and lots more!

Girls Know Best 2 is an incredible sequel filled with great advice and fun activities. It builds upon the success of the first book, but has developed its own personality with unique chapter ideas and forty-eight new girl authors from across the country. More fun from the people who really know—other girls!

152 pages, black and white collage art, $8.95 softcover

NOW LET'S HEAR FROM THE BOYS!

Finally, here is a great book written by boys! *Boys Know It All* is fun to read yet tackles some serious issues facing boys today. Guys offer helpful advice for tough situations and unique ideas for filling free time. Includes chapters on how to make friends, get out of bad situations, tell jokes, be a good sport, and create comics!

"Don't be afraid to try something new. Have a little fun. Be creative. Dream." —Phillip and Andrew, 12-year-old authors

168 pages, black and white collage art, $8.95 softcover

HOW ARE *YOU* GOING TO ROCK THE WORLD?

Did you know that:
- Joan of Arc was only seventeen when she led the French troops to victory?
- Cristen Powell started drag racing at sixteen and is now one of the top drag racers in America?
- Wang Yani began painting at the age of three? She was the youngest artist ever to have her own exhibit at the Smithsonian museum!

Get to know these incredible teen-age girls and many more in *Girls Who Rocked the World*. This is the first book ever to set girls' history straight by applauding inspiring young heroines.

125 pages, black and white interior, $8.95 softcover

TO ORDER ANY OF THE BOOKS LISTED HERE OR TO REQUEST A CATALOG, PLEASE SEE THE ORDER FORM ON THE FOLLOWING PAGE.

ORDER FORM

Name

Address

City   State/Province   Zip/Postal Code

Country

Phone Number

Title	Quantity	Price	Line Total

❑ Check if you would like
   us to include our catalog.

Subtotal	
Shipping (see below)	
Total	

We accept Visa, MasterCard, and American Express, or send a check or money order payable to Beyond Words Publishing.

Credit Card Number   Exp. Date

Shipping Rates (within the United States only)

First book: $3.00   Each additional book: $1.00

Please call for rates for special shipping services (overnight or international).

SEND THIS ORDER FORM TO:
Beyond Words Publishing, Inc.
20827 NW Cornell Road, Suite 500
Hillsboro, OR 97124-9808
or contact us via phone: 1-800-284-9673
in Oregon (503) 531-8700
fax: (503) 531-8773
email: sales@beyondword.com